HAFIZ

—

THE MYSTIC POETS

HAFIZ

—

THE MYSTIC POETS

Translated and with notes by Gertrude Bell

Preface by Ibrahim Gamard,
annotator and translator, *Rumi and Islam:
Selections from His Stories, Poems, and Discourses—
Annotated & Explained*

Walking Together, Finding the Way
SKYLIGHT PATHS Publishing
Woodstock, Vermont

Hafiz:
The Mystic Poets

2004 First Printing
© 2004 by SkyLight Paths Publishing

For information regarding permission to reprint material from this book, please write or fax your request to SkyLight Paths Publishing, Permissions Department, at the address / fax number listed below, or e-mail your request to permissions@skylightpaths.com.

Library of Congress Cataloging-in-Publication Data
Hāfiz, 14th cent.
[Dīvān. English. Selections]
Hafiz / translated and with notes by Gertrude Bell; with a preface
by Ibrahim Gamard
p. cm.—(The mystic poets series)
ISBN 1-59473-009-1
1. Sufi poetry, Persian—Translations into English. I. Bell, Gertrude
Lowthian, 1868–1926. II. Gamard, Ibrahim. III. Title. IV. Series.
PK6465.Z31 B4 2004
891'.5511—dc22

2003026092

10   9   8   7   6   5   4   3   2   1
Manufactured in Canada

SkyLight Paths Publishing is creating a place where people of different spiritual traditions come together for challenge and inspiration, a place where we can help each other understand the mystery that lies at the heart of our existence.

SkyLight Paths sees both believers and seekers as a community that increasingly transcends traditional boundaries of religion and denomination—people wanting to learn from each other, *walking together, finding the way.*

SkyLight Paths, "Walking Together, Finding the Way" and colophon are trademarks of LongHill Partners, Inc., registered in the U.S. Patent and Trademark Office.

Walking Together, Finding the Way
Published by SkyLight Paths Publishing
A Division of LongHill Partners, Inc.
Sunset Farm Offices, Route 4, P.O. Box 237
Woodstock, VT 05091
Tel: (802) 457-4000   Fax: (802) 457-4004
www.skylightpaths.com

Contents

Image: www.persianpaintings.com

Preface

Ibrahim Gamard

Hafiz became famous a century after the death of Jalaluddin Rumi, who often composed poems spontaneously in a state of spiritual ecstasy and did not seek formal perfection. Hafiz, in contrast, combined loftiness of meaning with perfection of form: he rewrote and polished his poems to the highest standards, discarding those that were less than he desired. This is one reason why he is considered the most loved poet of Persian speakers. Hafiz's works have been less well known to English-speaking readers, however. Only recently have I begun to appreciate his greatness—especially the exquisite manner in which he portrayed the same themes and metaphors of lover-Beloved mysticism that I love so much in the poems of Rumi and other masters of Persian Sufi poetry. I have also been struck by the wonderful musicality and frequent internal rhymes of his verse in Persian. One night I read an ode, or *ghazal,* to my wife, who commented on its elegance—simply upon hearing the sounds of the syllables. The last verse of the poem is followed here by a transliteration of the Persian so that the reader may gain a sense of the rhythm:[1]

> Hafiz, you sang ghazals, and you pierced pearls *with delicate skill, so* come and recite sweetly! For the

heavens will scatter the *necklace* knotted *starry jewels of the* Pleiades *as a reward* for your verses.

gha-ZAL GOF-TEE vo-DOR SOF-TEE be-YAA VO
KHOOSH be-KHVAAN HAA-FEZ ke BAR NAZ-ME
toWAF-SHAA-NAD fa-LAK `AQ-DE so-RAY-YAA RAA

There has been a renewed interest in Hafiz in recent years, but more than one American poet has published versions of Hafiz's poems that are not accurate translations from Persian of his imagery, thoughts, and wisdom. These versions resemble the popularized versions of Rumi's poetry created by other contemporary poets. Such authors do not read Persian and use translations made by Persian scholars as a basis or inspiration for their interpretive poetic versions.

In some ways, we should be thankful to such version-makers because they have had such success in making the names of great Persian poets such as Hafiz and Rumi, who lived more than seven hundred years ago, so well known in our time. Today, more readers than ever before are now interested in obtaining more accurate renderings of classical Persian poetry in English. While such readers have enjoyed the easy-to-read and entertaining versions, they also have felt deeply moved in their hearts by numerous metaphors and images of divine love and beauty. They became "thirsty" enough to seek to understand, on a deeper level, the genuine wisdom and beauty conveyed by these spiritual geniuses, for great literature translated from another language cannot be adequately appreciated without making effort. As Jalaluddin Rumi said, quoting from the Qur'an:

> If you say, "Purity *of heart* is *given* by the Kindness of God," the attainment of polishing *the heart* is also from that *divine* generosity.
>   *Since the reward of* that effort and prayer is *in accordance with* the amount of *a person's* determination and aspiration: "There is no *benefit* for man but what he strives for" (Q. 53:39).

Writing in 1947, A. J. Arberry, the well-known British scholar and translator of Rumi, described Gertrude Bell as "Hafiz's most felicitous translator." Although her translations, published in England in 1897, appear Victorian in style to the contemporary reader, they have very pleasing rhymes and rhythms, and are very rewarding to read. In spite of some loss of accuracy caused by the requirements of rhyme, her translations are much truer to the original than contemporary "versions" of Hafiz. Here is how she translated what Arberry called "one of the loveliest lines in Hafiz":

> Perhaps the tulip knows the fickleness
> Of Fortune's smile, for on her stalk's green shaft
> She bears a wine-cup through the wilderness.

Compare this to a literal translation followed by a transliteration of the original Persian, which may convey something of the original rhythm:

Perhaps the tulip has known about the faithlessness of the World, since she never put the cup of wine from (her) hand from birth until passing (away).

ma-GAR ke LA-la be-DAAN-AST(eh) BEE-wa-FAA-'iy-ye DAHR ke TAA be-ZAAD-o be-SHOD JAAM-e MAY ze-KAF na-ne-HAAD

Of course we need to understand that "wine" in Sufi Persian poetry usually does not mean an alcoholic beverage (forbidden in Islam) but has a wealth of spiritual meanings, such as the drunken bliss of Love that comes from the grace of God transmitted through the "wine-server," who often symbolizes the beloved spiritual Sufi master. Ambiguity is a major characteristic of Persian poetry, and Hafiz was one of the greatest masters of this artistic quality: each reader tends to see his or her own experiences reflected in the poems. As a result, it is usually unclear whether in a given verse he means actual wine or spiritual wine, a male or a female beloved, a human beloved or God, and so forth.

Khwaja Shamsu 'd-din Muhammad Hafiz was known as the "Tongue of the Invisible World" (Lisanu 'l-Ghayb), and he gives many indications of being a Sufi, a Muslim mystic:

I am seeing the Light of God in the tavern of the Zoroastrians. This is amazing—look at what light I am seeing from such a place!
O prince of the Pilgrimage *to the Ka'ba in Mecca,*

don't offer me *a description of* splendor! *Since* you see
only a building, and I am seeing the God of *that* House.

Sufism is not separate from Islam. Sufism is the
mystical dimension of Islam and has much in common
with Christian and Jewish mysticism. One would never
hear a claim, for example, that Hasidic mysticism was
separate from Judaism. Yet it is a popular belief that
Sufism is a kind of universal mysticism that is independ-
ent of any particular religion. Many Orientalists of the
past have presented this view, as do many popular "Sufi"
groups in Western countries at the present time.
However, during the past thirty years, many Western
scholars of Sufism have acknowledged that Sufism is the
mystical dimension of Islam and that Sufis are devout
Muslims who have mystical teachings that are harmo-
nious with the Islamic revelation.

Islamic mysticism began with the extraordinary spir-
itual experiences of the Prophet Muhammad. Small gath-
erings of Muslim mystics began to form during the first
centuries of Islam, often as a reaction to the worldly suc-
cess of the first Muslim empires. Sufi teachings developed
that initially stressed the importance of ascetic practices,
purification of the heart, cultivation of virtues, and pious
reverential awe toward God. Over time, more mystical
teachings developed, such as about the transcendence of
God beyond the universe as well as the immanence of
God within the creation, which mirrors the divine
Attributes—especially the saintly human being.

Mystical interpretations of verses from the Qur'an began early on. Some verses especially loved by Muslim Sufis are: "There is no divinity except God" (47:19); "Remember God standing, sitting down, and *lying down* on your sides" (4:103); "O men, you are poor in relation to God and God is the Rich" (35:15); "Whichever way you turn, there is the Face of God" (2:115); "God is the Light of the heavens and the earth" (24:35); "To God we belong and to Him we will return" (2:156); "And He is with you wherever you are" (57:4).

In addition, Sufis have long had a special love for certain sayings uttered by the Prophet Muhammad, or later attributed to him, such as: "Truly, for everything there is a polishing, and the polishing for the heart is the recollection of God"; [God said] "My earth does not contain Me, nor do My Heavens, but the heart of my believing servant contains Me"; [God said] "I was a Hidden Treasure, and then I loved that I might be known, and then I created the creation so that I might be known."

Unlike Rumi, Hafiz preferred not to mention such verses and sayings directly. For example, he used wine imagery to allude to the story of Adam's creation (Q. 2:30) and how humankind agreed to bear the burden of the divine "Trust" (Q. 33:72), sustained and strengthened (as he suggests) by an inward spiritual "wine," in verses which Gertrude Bell translated:

> Last night I dreamed that angels stood without
> The tavern door, and knocked in vain, and wept;

> They took the clay of Adam, and, methought,
> Moulded a cup therewith while all men slept.
> O dwellers in the halls of Chastity!
> You brought Love's passionate red wine to me,
> Down to the dust I am, your bright feet stepped.

The name "Hafiz" means "memorizer" and indicates that he memorized the entire Qur'an and must have been strongly influenced by it. As he said:

> *I swear* by the Qur'an that you retain in your heart, Hafiz, *that* I haven't seen *anything* sweeter than your poetry.

The great ninth-century Sufi Rabi'a of Basra enriched Sufism by her prayers such as "O God! If I worship You from fear of Hell, burn me in Hell. And if I worship with hope of Paradise, make *it* forbidden to me. But if I worship You for Your sake *alone,* do not withhold from me *Your* everlasting Beauty!" Hafiz expressed this same yearning in his own provocative way:

> If the hope of the ascetic is for the maidens and palaces *of Paradise* (Q. 55:72), for us the wine tavern is a palace and the beloved is a heavenly maiden.
>
> Drink wine with the sound of the harp and don't grieve. And if anyone says to you, "Don't drink wine," say, "God is the Forgiver" (Q. 10:107; 39:53).

Here, it should be noted that Hafiz was a particular kind of Sufi who deliberately sought the blame of the religious authorities, whom he criticized as arrogant hypocrites. There were, generally, two such types of Sufis: the *malamati,* who was secretly pious but outwardly nonconforming to the conventionally expected behavior of a religious person; and the *qalandar,* who spoke and behaved outrageously in public and disdained private piety as well (often claiming to have attained the final stages of the mystical path and, therefore, to have no need of prayer). Hafiz called himself a *rend*—similar to the first type: outwardly, he cultivated a bad reputation while inwardly pursuing his own unique spiritual quest. The purpose of seeking blame in Sufism is to counter the desire for a pious reputation, which often leads to hypocrisy. Therefore, Hafiz depicted himself as a "wine-worshipper," meaning a seeker of spiritual ecstasy; as a disciple of a "Zoroastrian priest," meaning a Sufi spiritual master (Zoroastrians were allowed to sell wine); as a "tavern-dweller," meaning someone who spends time in dervish gathering places.

> O *Sufi* shaykh, don't speak badly of *rend* people and be aware that *with this attitude* you are maintaining hatred for the Love of God.

This blame-seeking outlook enabled Hafiz to criticize religious authorities and Sufis, theologists and philosophers, ascetics and hedonists—while identifying only with scorned "drunkards." This explains why he portrayed himself so provocatively

> Stain the prayer carpet with wine if the Zoroastrian spiritual master tells you, since the *spiritual* seeker is

not unaware of the *Sufi* Path and the prescribed rules of *higher spiritual* levels.

Don't look for worship, faithful promises, and virtue from me, a drunkard—because I became disreputable by emptying *wine* cups *since* the Day of the Primordial Covenant *with God* (Q. 7:172).

The same moment that I made my ritual washing (for prayer) from the fountain of Love, I said "God is Most Great!" four times immediately (as a funeral prayer) over (the corpse of) everything that exists.

...O worshipper of wine, don't be despairing of the Mercy *of God* (Q.39:53).

If one reads many of the poems of Hafiz, it is easy to conclude that he drank actual wine (and many Iranian scholars are said to hold this view). However, it is quite possible that Hafiz deliberately portrayed himself in a convincing manner as a "wine-addict" as part of the blame-seeking path he followed. In some verses, he clearly spoke of "wine" as a spiritual symbol:

Drunkenness with the juice of a few grapes is not my manner *of conduct. Rather,* I am nurtured *and* aged *in* a "tavern."

Since the drunkenness of Love is not in your head, go *away,* since you are *only* a drunkard *from the wine* of grape juice.

Hafiz specialized in composing the *ghazal* form of poetry, which is usually between five and twelve lines in length; each line has two halves, and the last syllable or syllables of all the second halves of the lines rhyme. All the lines of a particular *ghazal* follow the same meter. The *ghazal,* which has been compared to an ode or a sonnet, usually focuses on themes of love and ideal beauty. This form of poetry can be initially difficult for the Western reader to relate to, since each line is usually independent of the preceding and following lines, so that there is no clear direction or conclusion in the poems. As mentioned previously, there is such ambiguity of meanings that it is unclear if a given poem is about worldly pleasures or spirituality, dissolute alcoholism or mysticism, a human beloved or God. But after reading the same images over and over in ever-changing contexts, one gradually leaves behind the ordinary material world and enters into a realm in which everything symbolizes the beautiful qualities of the beloved, who ultimately is God and the source of Love.

As the late German scholar Annemarie Schimmel wrote: "Persian poetry—from its very beginning conducive to precious, gemlike images—was the ideal vehicle to express these feelings [of enraptured mystical love]. The subtle harmony and ultimate equilibrium between the different spheres of being is best maintained in the poetry of Hafiz, whose verses are the perfect flower of the gardens of Shiraz, transparent as the air of that town, and fragrant as rose oil distilled from the centuries-old tradition of love of the divine revealed in visible forms."[2]

Who Is Hafiz?

Hafiz (ca. 1320–1389), whose name means "memorizer or reciter of the Qur'an," Islam's holy book, is known throughout the world as Persia's greatest poet. Although his work is still relatively unknown in America, sales of Hafiz's poems in modern Iran today rival sales of the Qur'an itself.

We do not know much about the life of Hafiz (usually pronounced HA-FEES in English), but we know that he lived in difficult times. Gertrude Bell, the translator of these poems, tells us: "His delicate love-songs were chanted to the rude accompaniment of the clash of arms, and his dreams must have been interrupted often enough by the nip of famine in a beleaguered town, the inrush of conquerors, and the flight of the defeated."

Hafiz never traveled far from his homeland; he was born, and later died, in Shiraz, located in modern Iran. We know that he was paid generously for his verses during his lifetime, but we also know that he died a poor man. He was married and had a son, but he outlived them both. He was a Sufi, a member of what was and still is a mystical movement within Islam, and he was known to his contemporaries by many reverential but mysterious titles, including "Tongue of the Hidden" and "Interpreter of Secrets."

The Time and Place in Which He Lived: Excerpts from Gertrude Bell's Original Preface to the Poems of Hafiz

Persia in the Fourteenth Century

The history of Persia in the fourteenth century is exceedingly confused. Beyond a succession of wars and turmoils, there is little to be learned concerning the political conditions under which Hafiz lived. Fifty years before the birth of the poet, Hulagu, a grandson of the great Tatar invader Genghis Khan, had conquered Baghdad, putting to death the last of the Abbasid caliphs and extinguishing the direct line of the race that had ruled over Persia since 750. For the next two hundred years there is indeed a branch of the family of Abbas living in Cairo, members of which were set up as caliphs by the Mamluk sultans of Egypt; but they were destitute of any real authority, and their position was that of dependents in the Mamluk court.

The sons and grandsons of Hulagu succeeded him as lords of Persia and Mesopotamia, paying a nominal allegiance to the Great Khan of the Mongols in Peiping or Peking [now Beijing], but for all practical purposes independent, and the different provinces of their empire were administered by governors in their name. About the time of the birth of Hafiz, that is to say in the beginning of the fourteenth century, a certain Mahmud Shah Inju was governing the province of Fars, of which Shiraz is the capital, in the name of Abu Said, the last of the direct descendants of Hulagu. On the death of Mahmud Shah, Abu Said appointed Sheikh Hussein ibn Juban to the governorship of Fars, a lucrative and much-coveted post. Sheikh Hussein took the precaution of ordering the three sons of Mahmud Shah to be seized and imprisoned; but while they were passing through the streets of Shiraz in the hands of their captors, their mother, who accompanied them, lifted her veil and made a touching appeal to the people, calling upon them to remember the benefits they had received from their late ruler, the father of the three boys. Her words took instant effect; the inhabitants rose, released her and her sons, and drove Sheikh Hussein into exile. He, however, returned with an army supplied by Abu Said, and induced Shiraz to submit again to his rule.

In 1335, a year or two after these events, Abu Said died, and the power of the house of Hulagu crumbled away. There followed a long period of anarchy, which was brought to an end when Oweis, another descendant of Hulagu, seized the throne. He and his son Ahmed reigned in Baghdad until Ahmed was driven out by the invading army of Timur. But during the years of anarchy the authority of the sultan of Baghdad had been considerably curtailed. On Abu Said's death, Abu Ishac, one of the three sons of Mahmud Shah Inju who had so narrowly escaped from the hands of Sheikh Hussein, took possession of Shiraz and Isfahan, finally ousting his old enemy, while Muhammad ibn Muzaffar, who had earned a name for valor in the service of Abu Said, made himself master of Yezd.

From this time onward, the governors of the Persian provinces seem to have given a nominal allegiance now to the sultan of Baghdad, now to the more distant caliph. The position of Shiraz between Baghdad and Cairo must have resembled that of Venice between Rome and Constantinople, and, like Venice, she was obedient to neither lord.

Abu Ishac had not steered his bark into quiet waters. In 1340, Shiraz was besieged and taken by a rival Atabeg, and the son of Mahmud Shah was obliged to content himself with Isfahan. But in the following year he returned, captured Shiraz by a stratagem, and again established himself as ruler over all Fars. The remaining years of his reign are chiefly occupied with military expeditions against Yezd, where Muhammad ibn Muzaffar and his sons were building up a formidable power.

Abu Ishac, Hafiz's First Royal Patron

In 1352, determined to put an end to these attacks, Muhammad marched into Fars and laid siege to Shiraz. Abu Ishac, whose life was one of perpetual dissipation, redoubled his orgies in the face of danger. Uncertain of the fidelity of the people of Shiraz, he put to death all the inhabitants of two quarters of the town, and contemplated insuring himself of a third quarter in a similar manner. But these measures did not lead to the desired results. The chief of the threatened quarter got wind of the king's design and delivered up the keys of his gate to Shah Shudja, son of Muhammad ibn Muzaffar, and Abu Ishac was obliged to seek refuge a second time in Isfahan. Four years later, in 1357, he was given up to Muhammad, who sent him to Shiraz and, with a fine sense of dramatic fitness, had him beheaded in an open space before the ruins of Persepolis.

The Arab traveler Ibn Batuta, who visited Shiraz between the years 1340 and 1350, has left a description of its ruler: "Abu Ishac is one of the best sultans that can be found" (it must be confessed that the average of sultans was not very high in Ibn Batuta's time); "he is fair of face, imposing of presence, and his conduct is no less to be admired. His mind is generous, his character remarkable, and he is modest, although his power is great and his territories extensive. His army exceeds the number of thirty thousand men, Turks and Persians. The most faithful of his subjects are the inhabitants of Isfahan; but he fears the Shirazis, who are a brave people, not to be controlled by kings, and he will not trust them with arms."

Abu Ishac shared the passion of the age for letters and was anxious to be accounted a rival to the king of Delhi in his generosity to men of learning; "but," sighs Ibn Batuta, "how far is the earth removed from the Pleiades!" The Persian historian who describes Abu Ishac's execution quotes a quatrain which the Atabeg is supposed to have written while he was in prison:

Lay down thine arms when Fortune is thy foe,
'Gainst Heaven's wheel, Wrestler, try not a throw
Drink steadfastly the cup whose name is Death,
Empty the dregs upon the earth, and go.

So perished the first patron of Hafiz. (For more about Abu Ishac, see pp. 21–23.)

More Kings, Wars, and Turmoil during Hafiz's Time

From 1353 to 1393, when Timur conquered Shiraz for the second and last time, the greater part of Persia was ruled by members of the house of Muzaffar. Scarcely a year passed undisturbed by civil war, scarcely a year in which one of the sons or grandsons of Muhammad did not suffer imprisonment or worse ills at the hands of his brothers. Muhammad himself was the first to fall. Shah Shudja seized his father while he was reading the Qur'an aloud with a poet of his court, and caused him to be blinded. A few years later the grim life beat itself out against the prison walls of Ka'lah-i-Safid.

"Without just cause," sings Hafiz, "the victor of victors suffered imprisonment; guiltless, the mightiest head was laid low. He had overcome Shiraz and Tabriz and Iraq; at the last his own hour came. He who, in the eyes of the world, was the light he had kindled [i.e., Muhammad's son, Shah Shudja], through those eyes which had gazed victorious upon the world, thrust the hot iron." A stern and pitiless man was this Muhammad, brave in battle, wise in council, ardent in religion, but hard and cruel beyond measure, a perfidious friend and a relentless enemy. The Persian historian Lutfallah relates that on several occasions he had seen criminals brought before Muhammad while the amir was engaged in reading the Qur'an. Laying the book aside, he would draw his sword and kill the offenders as they stood, and then return unmoved to his devotions. Shah Shudja once asked his father whether he had killed a thousand men with his own hand. "No," replied Muhammad, "but I think that the number of them that I have slain must reach eight hundred."

After his death, Shah Shudja reigned in Shiraz. Shah Shudja died in the odor of sanctity. Ten holy men were with him continually, reading the Qur'an aloud from end to end each day. He left behind him a name renowned for courage and for liberality. He was a poet, after the fashion of kings, and from boyhood he could repeat the Qur'an by heart.

The son, whose future Shah Shudja had spent his last hours in assuring, was not to remain for long upon the throne bequeathed to him by his father. During his short reign, Zein-el-Abeddin was engaged in defending himself from the attacks of his cousin Mansur, but in 1388 he was obliged to flee before an enemy more terrible than any he had yet known. Timur, who for several years had been hovering upon the borders of Fars, over-ran southern Persia and took Shiraz. Zein-el-Abeddin sought refuge with Mansur, who repaid his confidence by imprisoning and blinding him. It must have been in the year 1388 that the celebrated interview between Hafiz and Timur took place, and not at the time of the second conquest of Shiraz in 1393. The confusion between the two dates has led several writers to doubt the truth of the story, since it is almost certain that the poet had died before 1393. Timur bestowed Shiraz upon Shah Yahya, uncle to Mansur and sometime governor to Yezd; but no sooner was the Tatar army called away by disturbances in the northern parts of the empire than Mansur overthrew his uncle and possessed himself of Shiraz.

Hafiz did not live to see the end of the drama, but the end was not far off. In 1393 Timur advanced with thirty thousand picked men against Mansur. The Muzaffar, with only three or four thousand men, twice charged into the heart of the Tatar force, and at one moment Timur's own life was in danger. Mansur, who was himself fighting in the thickest of the battle, sent a message back to the wings of his army, ordering them to support his desperate charge; but they did not obey his command. He fell fighting beneath the sword of Shah Rukh Mirza, Timur's son, leaving the conqueror to "march in triumph through Persepolis."

Courage was a quality in which the descendants of Muhammad ibn Muzaffar were not deficient, but among a race of soldiers Mansur seems to have been distinguished for his reckless bearing. He, too, like the other members of his family, was a patron of learning, and it is related that he used to distribute two hundred tomans daily among the poor scholars of Shiraz. Both on account of their popularity and of their bravery, Timur saw that there would be no peace for him in Shiraz while one member of the house of Muzaffar remained alive; Mansur's survivors were put to the sword.

Hafiz's Personal History

Through all these changes of fortune, Hafiz appears to have played the prudent, if rather unromantic part of the vicar of Bray.[1] The slender thread of his personal history is made up, for the most part, of more or less mythical anecdote. He was the son, according to one tradition, of a baker of Shiraz, in which city he was probably educated. The poet Jāmī says that he does not know under what Sufi doctor Hafiz studied. As a young man, however, he was one of the followers of Sheikh Mahmud Attar, who would seem to have been somewhat of a freelance among the learned men of Shiraz. Sheikh Mahmud did not give himself up completely to the contemplative life, but combined the functions of a teacher with those of a dealer in fruit and vegetables. "O disciple of the tavern!" sings Hafiz, "give me the precious goblet, that I may drink to the sheikh who has no monastery."

Sheikh Mahmud's attitude doubtless brought him under the condemnation of the stricter Sufis, of the disciples of a certain Sheikh Hassan Asrakpush in particular, who as the title of their master denotes, clad themselves only in blue garments, and declared that their minds were filled with heavenly desires, just as their bodies were clothed in the color of heaven. Hafiz falls foul of this rival school in several of his poems. "I am the servant," he says, "of all who scatter the dregs of the cup and are clothed in one color [that is, clothed in sincerity], but not of them whose bodies are clad in blue while black is the color of their heart." And again: "Give me not the cup until I have torn from my breast the blue robe," by which he means that he cannot receive the teachings of true wisdom until he has divested himself of the errors of the uninitiated.

From Sheikh Mahmud, perhaps, Hafiz learned a wholesome philosophy which enabled him to see through the narrow-minded asceticism of other religious teachers, whether Sufi or orthodox, and he was not unmindful of the debt he owed him. "My Gray-Beard," he sings, "who scatters the dregs of the wine, has neither gold nor power, but God has made him both munificent and merciful." And indeed, if he succeeded in unchaining the spirit of his disciple from useless prejudice, it may be admitted that the sheikh went far toward providing him with a good equipment for life.

Although he never submitted to any strict monastic rule, Hafiz assumed the dervish habit of which he speaks so contemptuously. We must suppose that he took the precaution, which he himself recommends, of washing it clean in the wine that Sheikh Mahmud provided for him; in other words, that he tempered his orthodoxy with the freer doctrines he had derived from his teacher. He also became a sheikh.

How he first revealed his inimitable gift of song is not known. There is a tradition that upon a certain day one of his uncles was engaged in composing a poem upon Sufism, and being but a mediocre poet, could get no further than the first line. Hafiz took up the sheet in his uncle's absence and completed the verse. The uncle was not a little annoyed; he bade Hafiz finish the poem, and at the same time cursed him and his works. "They shall bring insanity," he declared, "upon all that read them." People say that the curse still hangs over the *Divan* [his collected poems]; therefore let no one whose reason is not strongly seated venture to study the poet. Whatever were his beginnings, it was not long before the young man rose into high repute.

Abu Ishac was his first patron. "By the favor of the victorious standards of a king," says Hafiz, "I was uplifted like a banner among the makers of verse." There is a long poem addressed to Abu Ishac, in which he is called the king under whose feet the garden of his kingdom bursts into flower. "O great and holy!" cries the poet, "every man who is a servant of thine is uplifted so high that the stars of Gemini are but as his girdle."

Hafiz must have been in Shiraz when Abu Ishac was brought there, a prisoner, from Isfahan; he may even have witnessed his execution outside Persepolis. "Fate overtook him," he sighs, "all too speedily—alas for the violence and oppression in this world of pitfalls! Alas for the grace and the mercy that dwelt among us! Hast thou not heard, O Hafiz, the laugh of the strutting partridge? Little considered be the clutching talons of the falcon of death."

From the protection of Abu Ishac, Hafiz passed into that of Shah Shudja, but the relations between the two men seem to have been somewhat strained. Shah Shudja may have distrusted the loyalty of one to whom Abu Ishac had been so good a patron; moreover, he nursed a professional jealousy of Hafiz, being himself a writer of occasional verse. The historian Khondamir tells of an interview which cannot have increased the goodwill of either interlocutor toward the other. Shah Shudja reproached Hafiz with the discursiveness of his songs. "In one and the same," he said, "you write of wine, of Sufism, and of the object of your affections. Now this is contrary to the practice of the eloquent." "That which your majesty has deigned to speak," replied Hafiz (laying his tongue in his cheek, though Khondamir does not mention the fact), "is the essence of the truth; yet the poems of Hafiz enjoy a wide celebrity, whereas those of some other writers have not passed beyond the gates of Shiraz." But an occasional bandying of sharp speeches, in which the King usually came off second best, did little harm to a friendship which was based upon a marked correspondence in tastes. "Since the hour," declares Hafiz, "that the wine-cup received honor from Shah Shudja, Fortune has put the goblet of joy into the hand of all wine-drinkers"; and in several poems he welcomes

Shah Shudja's accession to the throne and the consequent removal of an edict against the drinking of wine: "The daughter of the grape has repented of her retirement; she went to the keeper of the peace [i.e. Shah Shudja] and received permission for her deeds. Forth came she from behind the curtain that she might tell her lovers that she has turned about."

Partly out of gratitude, partly with an eye to future favors, Hafiz proclaimed the glory of Shah Shudja, just as he had proclaimed that of the hapless Abu Ishac, and the king was not averse from such good wishes as these from the most famous poet of the age: "May the ball of the heavens be for ever in the crook of thy polo stick, and the whole world be a playing-ground unto thee. The fame of thy goodness has conquered the four quarters of the earth; may it be for all time a guardian unto thee!"

One of Shah Shudja's viziers, Hadji Kawameddin Hassan, was also a good friend to Hafiz. In the poems he is frequently alluded to as the second Assaf (the first Assaf having been King Solomon's vizier, renowned for his wisdom), while Shah Shudja masquerades under the title of Solomon himself. On his return from a journey, probably to Yezd, Hafiz spent some months in the house of the vizier—induced thereto by a cogent argument. In one of the poems there is a dialogue between himself and a friend, in which the friend says to him, "When after two years' absence thy destiny has brought thee home, why comest thou not out of thy master's house?" Hafiz replies that the road in which he walks is not of his choosing: "An officer of my judge stands, like a serpent, in ambush upon the path, and whenever I would pass beyond my master's threshold he serves me with a summons and hurries me back into my prison." He goes on to remark that under these painful circumstances he finds his master's house a sure refuge, and the servants of the vizier useful allies against the officers of the law. "If any one proffers a demand to me there, I call to my aid the strong arm of one of the vizier's dependents, and with a blow I cause his skull to be cleft in two." A summary manner, one would think, of dealing with the law, and little calculated to incline the heart of his judge toward the offender.

There is another Kawameddin who is frequently mentioned, the vizier of Sultan Oweis of Baghdad. He founded in Shiraz a college for Hafiz, in which the poet gave lectures on the Qur'an and read out his own verses, and where his fame drew a great number of pupils. We find Hafiz asking his benefactor for money to support this school in the following terms: "O discreet friend [my poem], in some retired spot to which even the wind is a stranger, come to the ear of the master, and between jest and earnest place the pointed saying, that his heart may consent unto it; then, of thy kindness, pray his munificence to tell me, if I were to ask for a small stipend, would my request be tolerated?" One cannot but hope that so charming a begging letter, couched in verse, was more than tolerated. It was probably this vizier who sent a robe of honor to Hafiz, which, when it came, proved to be too short for him; "but," says the poet politely, "no favor of thine could be too short for any man."

From Oweis himself Hafiz is said to have received kindness, but he does not seem to have been satisfied with the sultan's conduct toward him: "From my heart," he says, "I am the slave of Sultan Oweis, but he remembers not his servant." The son of Oweis, Sultan Ahmed of Baghdad, whose cruelty caused his subjects to call in the aid of Timur against him, was very anxious to induce Hafiz to visit his court; but Hafiz, perhaps with prudence, declined the invitation, saying that he was content with dry bread eaten at home, and had no desire to taste the honey that pilgrims gather by the roadside. He sent to Ahmed a poem in which he loaded his name with extravagant praise. "O Persian soil," he declared, "the bud of joy has never blown for me. How excellent is the Tigris of Baghdad and the perfumed wine! O wind of the dawn, bring unto me the dust from my friend's threshold, that Hafiz may wash bright with it the eyes of his heart."

Once only did he comply with the invitations of foreign kings, and his experience on that occasion was far from encouraging. He visited Shah Yahya, Shah Shudja's brother, at Yezd, but the reward which he received was not commensurate with his expectations. "Long life to thee and thy heart's desire, O Cup-bearer of Djem's court!" he writes—and the context shows that the allusion is to Shah Yahya—"though while I dwelt with thee my cup was never filled with wine."

Moreover, a devoted lover of Shiraz, Hafiz was overcome with homesickness when he was absent from his native town. "Why," he says in a pathetic little poem written while he was at Yezd—"Why should I not return to mine own home? Why should I not lay my dust in the street of mine own beloved? My bosom cannot endure the sorrows of exile; let me return to mine own city; let me be master of my heart's desire." It was after this luckless visit to Shah Yahya that he is said to have remarked, "It seems that Fortune did not intend kings to be wise."

He never again gathered the honey of the roads of pilgrimage. Once in answer to the pressing invitation of Shah Mahmud Purabi, sultan of Bengal, he set forth for India, but a series of accidents befell him; he lost heart and returned home again.

From the sultan of Hormuz he received many favors, though he refused to visit him and his pearl fisheries in the Persian Gulf. He compares this sultan with Shah Yahya, much to the disadvantage of the latter, saying that the king who had never seen him had filled his mouth with pearls, whereas Shah Yahya, to whose court he had journeyed, had sent him empty away.

Shah Shudja was not the only member of the house of Muzaffar who protected Hafiz; the warrior prince Mansur was his staunch friend. He appears to have been absent from Shiraz at the time of Mansur's accession— perhaps he had accompanied Timur's retreating army. "The wind has brought me word," he cries, "that the day of sorrow is overpast; I will return to Shiraz through the favor of my friend. On the banners of the Conqueror [i.e. Mansur] Hafiz is borne up into heaven; fleeing for refuge, his destiny has set him upon the steps of a throne." Mansur held the poet in high esteem. There is a tradition that when he appointed one of his sons governor over a province, the young man asked his father to give him his vizier, Jelaleddin, as a counselor, and Hafiz as a teacher. "What!" replied Mansur, "would thou be king even in thy father's lifetime, that thou demands of him the two wisest men in his realm?"

Hafiz by this time had grown old. Youth had been very pleasant; not without a sigh the gray-haired man relinquished it. "Ah, why has my black hair turned white!" he laments, and tries to warm his old blood with the wine of former days. "Yesterday at dawn I came upon one or two glasses of wine—as sweet as the lip of the Cup-bearer they seemed to my palate. And then, my brain afire, I desired to return to my mistress, Youth, but between us a divorce had been pronounced." And again: "Last night Hafiz strayed into the tavern, and it seemed to him that Youth, his mistress, had come back, and that love and madness had returned to his old head."

Whether or not Hafiz lived to witness the overthrow of the race that had sheltered him, he foresaw the troubles that were coming upon it and upon his beloved Shiraz. There is a short poem full of foreboding, which is said to have been written after the entry of Timur: "What tumult I see beneath the moon's orbit; every quarter of the earth is full of evil and wickedness! There is strife among our daughters, and among our mothers contention, and the father is evilly disposed toward his son.

Only the foolish are drinking sherbet of rose-water and sugar; the wise are nourished upon their own heart's blood. The Arabian horse is wounded beneath the saddle, and the ass wears a collar of gold about his neck. Master, take the counsel of Hafiz: 'Go and do good!' for I see that this maxim is worth more than a treasure-house of jewels." In several verses he congratulates Mansur upon a victory and a fortunate return to Shiraz, which may perhaps refer to the re-establishment of the Muzaffarid line after Timur's departure. "Give me the cup," he says in one of these, "for the airs of youth blow through my old head, so glad am I to see the King's face again."

His Reputation after Death

The date of his death is variously given as 1388, 1389, 1391, and 1394, but it seems unlikely that he should have been alive as late as 1394. The year 1389 is given in a couplet by an unknown author, which is inscribed upon his tomb: "If thou would know when he sought a home in the dust of Mosalla, seek his date in the dust of Mosalla." The letters of the Persian words Khak-i-Mosalla, "dust of Mosalla," give the number 791; that is 1389 of our era. He lies in the garden of Mosalla outside Shiraz, a garden the praises of which he was never tired of singing, and on the banks of the Ruknabad, where he had so often rested under the shade of cypress trees. When, some sixty years after the poet's death, Sultan Baber conquered Shiraz, he erected a monument over the tomb of Hafiz. An oblong block of stone, on which are carved two songs from the Divan, marks the grave. At the head of it is inscribed a sentence in Arabic: "God is the enduring, and all else passes away." The garden contains the tombs of many devout Persians who have desired to rest in the sacred earth which holds the bones of the poet, and his prophecy that his grave should become a place of pilgrimage for all the drunkards of the world has been to a great extent fulfilled. A very ancient cypress, said to be of Hafiz's own planting, stood for many hundreds of years at the head of his grave and "cast its shadow o'er the dust of his desire."

It is not often that a teacher and the favorite of princes enjoys unmixed popularity, especially when his criticisms of such as disagree with him are as harsh and as often repeated as are those of Hafiz; nor does he seem to have been an exception to the general rule. Moreover, his own conduct gave his enemies sufficient grounds for complaint. His biographers, as biographers will, take a rosy view of his life. Daulat Shah, for instance, states that "he turned always to the company of dervishes and of wise men, and sometimes he attained also to the society of princes; a friend of persons of eminent virtue and perfection, and of noble youths." But such accounts as these are not entirely borne out by other traditions, and his poems do not seem to the unbiased reader to be the works of a man of ascetic temperament. With all due deference to Daulat Shah, I would submit that Abu Ishac, Shah Shudja, and Shah Mansur were none of them persons of eminent virtue; indeed, it is difficult to imagine that a friend and panegyrist of theirs could have renounced all the joys of life.

His enemies went so far as to accuse him of heresy and even of atheism, and so strong was popular feeling against him that, on his death, it was debated whether his body might be given the rites of burial. The question was settled only by consulting his poems, which, on being taken at haphazard, opened upon the following verse: "Fear not to follow with pious feet the corpse of Hafiz, for though he was drowned in the ocean of sin, he may find a place in paradise." It is a fortunate age which will allow a person's writings to stand his doubtful reputation in such good stead.

It is not only as a maker of exquisite verse but also as a philosopher that Hafiz has gained so wide an esteem in the East. No Westerner who reads his *Divan* but will be taken captive by the delicious music of his songs, the delicate rhythms, the beat of the refrain, and the charming imagery. Some of them are instinct with the very spirit of youth and love and joy; some have a nobler humanity and cry out across the ages with a voice pitifully like our own; and yet few of us will turn to Hafiz for wisdom and comfort, or choose him as a guide. It is the interminable, the hopeless mysticism, the playing with words that say one thing and mean something totally different, the vagueness of a philosophy that dares not speak out, which repels the Western just as much as it attracts the Oriental mind. "Give us a working theory," we demand. "Build us imaginary mansions where our souls, fugitives from the actual, may dream themselves away"—that, it seems to me, is what the Persian asks of his teacher.

Gertrude Bell made her selections from Hafiz's complete collection of poems, known as the *Divan,* and prepared these translations. Each of the poems reproduced here is from Bell's original selection, but not necessarily in the order in which she first published them. Bell did not title the poems, but the editors have added titles for this edition. Each title is followed by the original number given it by Bell, for the convenience of those readers who may want to make reference to earlier editions.

A Short Introduction
to Hafiz's Mysticism

Sufism is a mysticism inspired by the holy book of Islam, the Qur'an, although according to many Sufis its spirit has lived in the hearts of people since the beginning of time. Sufism as a mystical movement arose within religion in the teachings of the Prophet Muhammad and grew out of the roots of Islam. One tenth-century Sufi mystic explained: "Today Sufism is a name without a reality, but formerly it was a reality without a name." A later mystic added: "In the time of the Companions [of the Prophet] and their successors this name did not exist, but the reality thereof was in everyone; now the name existeth, but not the reality."[1]

Sufism is the inner path, the way of discovering hidden meaning in the universe, a journey to union with the Divine.

Laleh Bakhtiar summarizes the beliefs of Sufism in this way:

> Sufis recognize both the immanence and the transcendence of God at one and the same time, and express this in their doctrine. At the same time as God is immanent, God is absolutely transcendent. At the same time as God is "nearer … than the jugular vein" (Qur'an 50:16), God is above every form, thought, or thing in the universe, as described in the

Throne Verse (2:256). There is a coincidence of opposites here which can be known only through the Intellect or Spirit which shows itself to the mystic through spiritual intuition.[2]

This rich mystical tradition is also aptly summarized in the depths of meaning discovered in these two simple lines from the twentieth-century Sufi master Hazrat Inayat Khan. Khan explains the meaning of love between God and humankind through the simple and ancient Sufi metaphor of the moth being consumed in the flame of a candle:

Moth: "I gave you my life."
Flame: "I allowed you to kiss me."[3]

(See the Hafiz poem "Radiance Draws the Moth's Desire" on p. 94, as well.)

As Gertrude Bell explains above, Hafiz was himself a sheikh and a popular interpreter of the Qur'an and Sufi mysticism during his lifetime. His poems are full of Sufi imagery, and they demonstrate his overwhelming desire for union with the Divine, the primary goal of all Sufi teaching and life.

Sufism seeks a direct encounter with God, Allah, the Divine. The Sufi path is necessarily experiential, and it is possible today for someone to draw upon Sufi philosophy and be a participant in another religious tradition.

The Sufi way is to aim to experience God directly in one's life; this can happen within religion—or as an aid to deeper spiritual understanding within religion—or it can occur as a distinct path of its own. Past Orientalists such as Gertrude Bell did not see Sufism as a genuine expression of Islam, but contemporary Western scholars have now revised that view.

Most Sufis believe that the Prophet Muhammad was an exemplary Sufi himself. According to one tradition, "The Messenger of God [Muhammad] said: 'Piety is here,' and pointed with his hand to his heart."[4] Sufis emphasize the more mystical verses of the Qur'an, such as these:

"God has shown you his signs on the horizon and in your being." (41:53)

"O soul at peace, return unto thy Lord, well-pleased, well-pleasing.

Enter thou among My servants! Enter thou My Paradise!" (39:29)

"Repel not those who call upon their Lord in the morning and evening, seeking His countenance." (6:52)

For centuries, many Sufis were believed to have practiced their faith in solitude or secret. The most visible expression of Sufi spirituality, for example, is the ceremony of "whirling" practiced by dervishes in many of the Sufi orders. It has become known and experienced firsthand by non-Sufis in America only in the past half century.

The Beliefs and Spiritual Practices of Sufism: Excerpts from Gertrude Bell's Original Preface

Doctrines of Sufism

Hafiz belonged to the great sect from which so many of the most famous among Persian writers have sprung. Like Saadi and Jāmī and Jalal ad-Dīn Rūmī and a score of others, he was a Sufi.

The keynote of Sufism is the union, the identification of God and humanity. Numberless beautiful images are used to describe this union. Rūmī: "There came one and knocked at the door of the Beloved. And a voice answered and said, 'Who is there?' The lover replied, 'It is I.' 'Go hence,' returned the voice; 'there is no room within for thee and me.' Then came the lover a second time and knocked and again the voice demanded, 'Who is there?' He answered, 'It is thou.' 'Enter,' said the voice, 'for I am within.'"

It is a doctrine which lies at the root of all spiritual religions, but pushed too far it leads to pantheism, quietism, and eventually to nihilism. The highest good to which the Sufis can attain is the annihilation of the actual—to forget that they have a separate existence, and to lose themselves in the Divinity as a drop of water is lost in the ocean.

In order to obtain this end, they recommend ascetic

living and solitude; but they do not carry asceticism to the absurd extremes enjoined by the Indian mystics, nor do they approve of artificial aids for the subduing of consciousness, such as opium, or hashish, or the wild physical exertions of the dancing dervishes. The drunkenness of the Sufi poets, say their interpreters, is nothing but an ecstatic frame of mind, in which the spirit is intoxicated with the contemplation of God just as the body is intoxicated with wine.

According to the *Dabistan,* there are four stages in the manifestation of the Divinity: in the first the mystic sees God in the form of a corporal being; in the second he sees him in the form of one of his attributes of action, as the maker or the preserver of the world; in the third he appears in the form of an attribute which exists in his very essence, as knowledge or life; in the fourth the mystic is no longer conscious of his own existence. To the last he can hope to attain but seldom.

This losing of the soul in God is only a return (and here we come near to such Platonic doctrines as those embodied in the *Phaedrus*) to the conditions which existed before birth into the world. Just as in the Dialogue the immortal steed which is harnessed to the chariot of the soul longs to return to the plain of birth, and to see again the true justice, beauty, and wisdom of which it has retained an imperfect recollection, so the soul of the Sufi longs to return to God, from whom it has been separated by the mortal veil of the body. But this reunion is pushed much further by the Eastern philosophers than by Plato; it implies, according to them, the complete annihilation of distinct personality, corresponding to the conditions, quite unlike those described by the Platonic Socrates, which they believe to have existed before birth.

There is nothing which is not from God and a part of God. In himself he contains both being and not being; when he chooses he casts his reflection upon the void, and that reflection is the universe. There is a fine passage in Jāmī's Yusuf and Zuleikha in which he sets forth this doctrine of the creation. "Thou art but the glass," the poet concludes; "his is the face reflected in the mirror; nay, if thou lookest steadfastly, thou shalt see that he is the mirror also." In a parable, Jāmī illustrates the universal presence of God, and the blind searching of man for that by which he is surrounded on every side. There was a frog which sat upon the shores of the ocean, and ceaselessly day and night he sang its praise. "As far as mine eyes can see," he said, "I behold nothing but thy boundless surface." Some fish swimming in the shallow water heard the frog's song and were filled with a desire to find that wonderful ocean of which he spoke, but go where they would they could not discover it. At last, in the course of their search, they fell into a fisherman's net, and as soon as they were drawn out of the water they saw beneath them the ocean for which they had been seeking. With a leap they returned into it.

It has been well said that all religious teachers who have honestly tried to construct a working formula have found that one of their greatest difficulties lay in reconciling the all-powerfulness of God with the human consciousness of its being free; for on the one hand it is impossible to conceive a God worth the name who shall be less than omnipotent and omniscient, and on the other it is essential to lay upon us some responsibility for our actions.

Muhammad found himself confronted with this difficulty, since his primary object was to exalt the divine personality and to lift it out of the pantheism into which it had fallen among the pre-Islamitic Arabs; but if he did not succeed in indicating a satisfactory way out of the dilemma, it is at least unjust to accuse him of having failed to recognize it. He insisted that humanity is responsible for its own salvation: "Whoever chooses the life to come, their desire shall be acceptable to God." (St. Paul is scarcely more explicit: "Work out your own salvation; for it is God which works in you both to will and to work for his good pleasure" [Phil. 2:12].) There is a tradition that when some of his disciples were disputing over predestination, Muhammad said to them: "Why do you not imitate Omar? For when one came to him and asked him, 'What is predestination?' he answered, 'It is a deep sea.' And a second time he replied, 'It is a dark road.' And a third time, 'It is a secret which I will not declare, since God has seen fit to conceal.'"

There is neither good nor evil, since both flow from God, from whom all flows. Some go so far as to prefer Pharaoh to Moses, Nimrod to Abraham, because they say that though Pharaoh and Nimrod were in apparent revolt against the Divinity, in reality they knew their own nothingness and accepted the part that the divine wisdom had imposed upon them. There is neither reward nor punishment; Paradise is the beauty, Hell the glory, of God, and when it is said that those in Hell are wretched, it is meant that the dwellers in Heaven would be wretched in their place.

Finally, there is no distinction between God and humanity. The soul is but an emanation from God, and a person is therefore justified in saying with the fanatic Hallaj, who lived in the ninth century, "I am God." Hallaj was believed by some to be a sorcerer, and by others a holy worker of miracles. He was condemned to death with horrible tortures by the caliph of Baghdad in 919, and his ashes were thrown into the Tigris. It is said that a Sufi once asked God why he suffered his servant Hallaj to fall into the caliph's hands, and was answered, "Thus the revealers of secrets are punished." Though Hallaj paid with his life for venturing to give voice to his opinion, he was only repeating aloud what all Sufis believe to be true.

"It is permitted to a tree to say, 'I am God,'" writes the author of *Gulshen-i-Raz* (the allusion is to the burning bush that spoke to Moses); "why then may not a person say it?" And again: "In God there is no distinction of quality; in his divine majesty I, thou, and we shall not be found. I, thou, we, and he bear the same meaning, for in unity there is no division. Every person who has annihilated the body and is entirely separated from himself, hears within his heart a voice that crieth, 'I am God.'"

Sufi Beliefs and Other Religious Traditions

The conception of the union and interdependence of all things divine and human is far older than Sufi thought. It goes back to the earliest Indian teaching, and the conclusion which is drawn from it is in the Veda. "The gospels," Paul Deussen [professor of Indian philosophy who wrote about the Upanishads at the end of the nineteenth century] says, "fix quite correctly as the highest law of morality, Love thy neighbor as thyself. But why should I do so, since by the order of nature I feel pain and pleasure only in myself, not in my neighbor? The answer is not in the Bible, but it is in the Veda: You shall love your neighbor as yourselves because you are your neighbor; a mere illusion makes you believe that your neighbor is something different from yourselves."

"When thou and I remain not [when humanity is completely united with God], what matters the Ka'ba and the Synagogue and the Monastery?" *(Gulshen-i-Raz)*. That is, what difference is there between the religion of Muslim, Jew, and Christian? Ferideddin Attar tells this beautiful allegory:

One night the angel Gabriel was seated on the branches of a tree in the Garden of Paradise, and he heard God pronounce a word of assent. At this moment, thought the angel, someone is invoking God. I know not who he is; but this I know, that he must be a notable servant of the Lord, one whose soul is dead to evil and whose spirit lives. Then Gabriel desired to know who this person could be, but in the seven zones he found him not. He traversed the land and the sea and found him not in mountain or in plain. Therefore he hastened back to the presence of God, and again he heard him give a favorable answer to the same prayers. Again he set forth and sought through the world, yet he saw not the servant of God. "O Lord," he cried, "show me the path that leads to him upon whom thy favors fall!" "Go to the land of Rome," God answered, "and in a certain monastery you shall find him." There Gabriel fled and found him whom he sought, and lo! he was worshiping an idol. When he returned, Gabriel opened his lips and said, "O Master, draw aside for me the veil from this secret: why fulfill thou the prayers of one who invokes an idol in a monastery?" And God replied, "His spirit is darkened and he knows not that he has missed the way; but since he errs from ignorance, I pardon his fault: my mercy is extended to him, and I allow him to enter into the highest place."

The Sufis had no difficulty in finding in the Qur'an texts in support of their teaching. When Muhammad exclaims, "There are times when neither cherubim or prophet are equal to me!" the Sufis declare that he alludes to moments of ecstatic union with God. And his account of the victory of Bedr—"Thou did not slay them, but God slew them, and thou did not shoot when thou did shoot, but God shot"—they take as a proof of the Prophet's belief in the essential oneness of God and humanity. The whole book is twisted after this fashion into agreement with their views.

Beautiful and spiritual as some of these doctrines are, they can hardly be said to form an adequate guide to conduct. The Sufis, however, are regarded in the East as people leading a virtuous life and pure life. Even the etymology of their name points to the same conclusion: *Sufi* comes from an Arabic word signifying "wool" and indicates that they were accustomed to clothe themselves in simple woolen garments. They occupy in the East much the same position that Madame Guyon and the Jansenists occupied in the West. So far as the Sufis are striving earnestly after union with God, they are saved from the logical consequences of their doctrines: "Their ear is strained to catch the sounds of the lute, their eyes are fixed upon the cup, their bosoms are filled with the desire of this world and of the world to come" (Sayyed Ahmed of Isfahan). And in the same spirit Hafiz sings: "Though the winds of discord shake the two worlds, mine eyes are fixed upon the road from whence cometh my Friend." Most Sufis are good and religious men, holding it their duty to conform outwardly and to conceal from the orthodox the beliefs which they cherish in their heart, holding also that the practice of the religion of Islam, to which they have attached symbolic meanings, is the only way to the perfection to which they aspire.

The Poems

Fresh and New (10)

Singer, sweet Singer, fresh notes strew,
    Fresh and afresh and new and new!
Heart-gladdening wine thy lips imbrue,
    Fresh and afresh and new and new!

Saki, thy radiant feet I hail;
Flush with red wine the goblets pale,
Flush our pale cheeks to drunken hue,
    Fresh and afresh and new and new!

Then with thy love to toy with thee,
Rest thee, ah, rest! where none can see;
Seek thy delight, for kisses sue,
    Fresh and afresh and new and new!

Here round thy life the vine is twined;
Drink! for elsewhere what wine wilt find?
Drink to her name, to hours that flew,
    Hours ever fresh and new and new!

While he was alive, [Hafiz] was bitterly opposed by supposed "men
of the spirit," who denounced him as an infidel and libertine.
Unable to understand the allegorical nature of his work, they
assumed that it was blasphemous, dangerous, superficial, and
pornographic. Deeply conditioned to regard love and beauty as
appertaining to the lowest of human emotions—and consequently
themselves representing perverted minds—they often accused him
of perversion.—Idries Shah[2]

She that has stolen my heart from me,
How does she wield her empery?
Paints and adorns and scents her too,
    Fresh and afresh and new and new!

Wind of the dawn that passest by,
Swift to the street of my fairy hie,
Whisper the tale of Hafiz true,
    Fresh and afresh and new and new!

"The cup-bearer, *sāqī* causes one to drink; and it is the attention of
the *sāqī* that one seeks. The cup-bearer brings the wine of love and
affection, and symbolizes the Shaykh who guides one through love
to drink of Divine Knowledge."—Laleh Bakhtiar[1]

Where Is My Ruined Life? (12)

Where is my ruined life, and where the fame
    Of noble deeds?
Look on my long-drawn road, and whence it came,
    And where it leads!

Can drunkenness be linked to piety
    And good repute?
Where is the preacher's holy monody,
    Where is the lute?

From monkish cell and lying garb released,
    O heart of mine,
Where is the Tavern fane, the Tavern priest,
    Where is the wine?

Past days of meeting, let the memory
    Of you be sweet!
Where are those glances fled, and where for me
    Reproaches meet?

"The vast majority of [Hafiz's] work is said to have been destroyed
by clerics and rulers who disapproved of the content of his poems....
Hafiz was viewed as a great threat, a spiritual rebel, whose insights
emancipate his readers from the clutches of those in power.... For
Hafiz reveals a God with a billion I.Q.—a God that would never
cripple us with guilt or control us with fear."—Daniel Ladinsky[3]

His friend's bright face warms not the enemy
    When love is done—
Where is the extinguished lamp that made night day
    Where is the sun?

Balm to mine eyes the dust, my head I bow
    Upon thy stair.
Where shall I go, where from thy presence? thou
    Art everywhere.

Look not upon the dimple of her chin,
    Danger lurks there!
Where wilt thou hide, O trembling heart, fleeing, in
    Such mad haste—where?

To steadfastness and patience, friend, ask not
    If Hafiz keep—
Patience and steadfastness I have forgot,
    And where is sleep?

Please Take Care of My Heart (13)

Lady that hast my heart within thy hand,
Thou heed'st me not; and if thou turn thine ear
Unto the wise, thou shalt not understand—
Behold the fault is thine, our words were clear.
For all the tumult in my drunken brain
Praise God! who trieth not His slave in vain;
Nor this world nor the next shall make me fear!

My weary heart eternal silence keeps—
I know not who has slipped into my heart;
Though I am silent, one within me weeps.
My soul shall rend the painted veil apart.
Where art thou, Minstrel! touch thy saddest strings
Till clothed in music such as sorrow sings,
My mournful story from thy zither sweeps.

Lo, not at any time I lent mine ear
To hearken to the glories of the earth;
Only thy beauty to mine eyes was dear.
Sleep has forsaken me, and from the birth
Of night till day I weave bright dreams of thee;
Drunk with a hundred nights of revelry,
Where is the tavern that sets forth such cheer!

My heart, sad hermit, stains the cloister floor
With drops of blood, the sweat of anguish dire;
Ah, wash me clean, and o'er my body pour
Love's generous wine! the worshipers of fire

Have bowed them down and magnified my name,
For in my heart there burns a living flame,
Transpiercing Death's impenetrable door.

What instrument through last night's silence rang?
My life into his lay the minstrel wove,
And filled my brain with the sweet song he sang.
It was the proclamation of thy love
That shook the strings of Life's most secret lyre,
And still my breast heaves with last night's desire,
For countless echoes from that music sprang.

And ever, since the time that Hafiz heard
His Lady's voice, as from a rocky hill
Reverberates the softly spoken word,
So echoes of desire his bosom fill.

"Wine is a symbol for the ecstasy which causes the Sufi to be beside
himself when in the presence of a vision or emanation of the
Beloved. It is the symbol of the Absolute, manifested and present.
Wine is the catalyst which causes a motion between the mystic's
soul and the spiritual vision."—Laleh Bakhtiar[4]

Hafiz Can Lose No More (14)

The nightingale with drops of his heart's blood
Had nourished the red rose, then came a wind,
And catching at the boughs in envious mood,
A hundred thorns about his heart entwined.
Like to the parrot crunching sugar, good
Seemed the world to me who could not stay
The wind of Death that swept my hopes away.

Light of mine eyes and harvest of my heart,
And mine at least in changeless memory!
Ah, when he found it easy to depart,
He left the harder pilgrimage to me!
O Camel-driver, though the cordage start,
For God's sake help me lift my fallen load,
And Pity be my comrade of the road!

My face is seamed with dust, mine eyes are wet.
Of dust and tears the turquoise firmament
Kneadeth the bricks for joy's abode; and yet....
Alas, and weeping yet I make lament!
Because the moon her jealous glances set
Upon the bow-bent eyebrows of my moon,
He sought a lodging in the grave—too soon!

I had not castled, and the time is gone.
What shall I play? Upon the chequered floor
Of Night and Day, Death won the game—forlorn
And careless now, Hafiz can lose no more.

The Glow of My Love's Red Cheek (9)

O Cup-bearer, set my glass afire
With the light of wine! O minstrel, sing:
The world fulfilleth my heart's desire!
Reflected within the goblet's ring
I see the glow of my Love's red cheek,
And scant of wit, ye who fail to seek
The pleasures that wine alone can bring!

Let not the blandishments be checked
That slender beauties lavish on me,
Until in the grace of the cypress decked,
Love shall come like a ruddy pine-tree
He cannot perish whose heart doth hold
The life love breathes—though my days are told,
In the Book of the World lives my constancy.

But when the Day of Reckoning is here,
I fancy little will be the gain
That accrues to the Sheikh for his lawful cheer,
Or to me for the draught forbidden I drain.
The drunken eyes of my comrades shine,
And I too, stretching my hand to the wine,
On the neck of drunkenness loosen the rein.

O wind, if thou passest the garden close
Of my heart's dear master, carry for me
The message I send to him, wind that blows!
"Why hast thou thrust from thy memory
My hapless name?" breathe low in his ear;
"Knowest thou not that the day is near
When nor thou nor any shall think on me?"

If with tears, O Hafiz, thine eyes are wet,
Scatter them round thee like grain, and snare
The Bird of Joy when it comes to thy net.
As the tulip shrinks from the cold night air,
So shrank my heart and quailed in the shade;
O Song-bird Fortune, the toils are laid,
When shall thy bright wings lie pinioned there?

The heavens' green sea and the bark therein,
The slender bark of the crescent moon,
Are lost in thy bounty's radiant noon,
Vizier and pilgrim, Kawameddin!

No Reproach for the Drunkard (17)

Lay not reproach at the drunkard's door
O Fanatic, thou that are pure of soul;
Not thine on the page of life to enroll
The faults of others! Or less or more
I have swerved from my path—keep thou to thine own
For every man when he reaches the goal
Shall reap the harvest his hands have sown.

Leave me the hope of a former grace—
Till the curtain is lifted none can tell
Whether in Heaven or deepest Hell,
Fair or vile, shall appear his face.
Alike the drunk and the strict of fare
For his mistress yearns—in the mosque Love doth
        dwell
And the church, for his lodging is everywhere.

"Intoxicated ones, mastān, are lovers of God, Sufis who are
drowned in the sea of Unity, acquainted with mysteries but
unaware of the vicissitudes of this world."—Laleh Bakhtiar[5]

If without the house of devotion I stand,
I am not the first to throw wide the door;
My father opened it long before,
The eternal Paradise slipped from his hand.
All you that misconstrue my words' intent,
I lie on the bricks of the tavern floor,
And a brick shall serve me for argument.

Heaven's garden future treasures may yield—
Ah, make the most of earth's treasury!
The flickering shade of the willow-tree,
And the grass-grown lip of the fruitful field.
Trust not in deeds—the Eternal Day
Shall reveal the Creator's sentence on thee;
But till then, what His finger has writ, who can say.

Bring the cup in thine hand to the Judgment-seat;
Thou shalt rise, O Hafiz, to Heaven's gate
From the tavern where thou hast tarried late.
And if thou hast worshiped wine, thou shalt meet
The reward that the Faithful attain;
If such thy life, then fear not thy fate;
Thou shalt not have lived and worshiped in vain.

Come and Touch My Eyes (15)

Return! that to a heart wounded full sore
Valiance and strength may enter in; return!
And Life shall pause at the deserted door,
The cold dead body breathe again and burn.
Oh come! and touch mine eyes, of thy sweet grace,
For I am blind to all but to thy face.
Open the gates and bid me see once more!

Like to a cruel Ethiopian band,
Sorrow despoiled the kingdom of my heart—
Return! glad Lord of Rome, and free the land;
Before thine arms the foe shall break and part.
See now, I hold a mirror to mine eyes,
And nought but thy reflection therein lies;
The glass speaks truth to them that understand.

Night is with child, hast thou not heard men say?
"Night is with child! what will she bring to birth?"
I sit and ask the stars when thou'rt away.
Oh come! and when the nightingale of mirth
Pipes in the Spring-awakened garden ground,
In Hafiz's heart shall ring a sweeter sound,
Diviner nightingales attune their lay.

Love at Least Exists (16)

What is wrought in the forge of the living and life—
All things are nought! Ho! fill me the bowl,
For nought is the gear of the world and the strife!
One passion has quickened the heart and the soul,
The Beloved's presence alone they have sought—
Love at least exists; yet if Love were not,
Heart and soul would sink to the common lot—
    All things are nought!

Like an empty cup is the fate of each,
That each must fill from Life's mighty flood;
Nought thy toil, though to Paradise gate thou reach,
If Another has filled up thy cup with blood;
Neither shade from the sweet-fruited trees could be
        bought
By thy praying—O Cypress of Truth, dost not see
That Sidreh and Tuba were nought, and to thee
    All then were nought!

The span of thy life is as five little days,
Brief hours and swift in this halting-place;
Rest softly, ah rest! while the Shadow delays,
For Time's self is nought and the dial's face.
On the lip of Oblivion we linger, and short
Is the way from the Lip to the Mouth where we
        pass—
While the moment is thine, fill, O Saki, the glass
    Ere all is nought!

Consider the rose that breaks into flower,
Neither repines, though she fade and die—
The powers of the world endure for an hour,
But nought shall remain of their majesty.
Be not too sure of your crown, you who thought
That virtue was easy and recompense yours;
From the monastery to the wine-tavern doors
    The way is nought!

What though I, too, have tasted the salt of my tears,
Though I, too, have burnt in the fires of grief,
Shall I cry aloud to unheeding ears?
Mourn and be silent! nought brings relief.
Thou, Hafiz, art praised for the songs thou hast
        wrought,
But bearing a stained or an honored name,
The lovers of wine shall make light of thy fame—
    All things are nought!

Love Less Easy (1)

Arise, O Cup-bearer, rise! and bring
To lips that are thirsting the bowl they praise,
For it seemed that love was an easy thing,
But my feet have fallen on difficult ways.
I have prayed the wind o'er my heart to fling
The fragrance of musk in her hair that sleeps—
In the night of her hair—yet no fragrance stays
The tears of my heart's blood my sad heart weeps.

Hear the Tavern-keeper who counsels you:
"With wine, with red wine your prayer carpet dye!"
There was never a traveler like him but knew
The ways of the road and the hostelry.
Where shall I rest, when the still night through,
Beyond thy gateway, O Heart of my heart,
The bells of the camels lament and cry:
"Bind up thy burden again and depart!"

The waves run high; night is clouded with fears,
And eddying whirlpools clash and roar;
How shall my drowning voice strike their ears
Whose light-freighted vessels have reached the shore?
I sought mine own; the unsparing years
Have brought me mine own, a dishonoured name.
What cloak shall cover my misery o'er
When each jesting mouth has rehearsed my shame!

O Hafiz, seeking an end to strife,
Hold fast in thy mind what the wise have writ:
"If at last thou attain the desire of thy life,
Cast the world aside, yea, abandon it!"

Whispered Prayers (3)

Wind from the east, O Lapwing of the day,
I send thee to my Lady, though the way
Is far to Saba, where I bid thee fly;
Lest in the dust thy tameless wings should lie,
Broken with grief, I send thee to thy nest,
    Fidelity.

Or far or near there is no halting-place
Upon Love's road—absent, I see thy face,
And in thine ear my wind-blown greetings sound,
North winds and east waft them where they are
       bound,
Each morn and eve convoys of greeting fair
    I send to thee.

Unto mine eyes a stranger, thou that art
A comrade ever-present to my heart,
What whispered prayers and what full meed of praise
    I send to thee.

Lest Sorrow's army waste thy heart's domain,
I send my life to bring thee peace again,
Dear life thy ransom! From thy singers learn
How one that longs for thee may weep and burn;
Sonnets and broken words, sweet notes and songs
    I send to thee.

Give me the cup! a voice rings in mine ears
Crying: "Bear patiently the bitter years!
For all thine ills, I send thee heavenly grace.
God the Creator mirrored in thy face
Thine eyes shall see, God's image in the glass
    I send to thee.

Hafiz, thy praise alone my comrades sing;
Hasten to us, thou that art sorrowing!
A robe of honor and a harnessed steed
    I send to thee."

Hafiz, Your Heart! (4)

Sleep on thine eyes, bright as narcissus flowers,
    Falls not in vain!
And not in vain thy hair's soft radiance showers—
    Ah, not in vain!

Before the milk upon thy lips was dry,
    I said: "Lips where the salt of wit doth lie,
Sweets shall be mingled with thy mockery,
    And not in vain!"

Thy mouth the fountain where life's waters flow,
    A dimpled well of tears is set below,
And death lies near to life thy lovers know,
    But know in vain!

God send to thee great length of happy days!
    Lo, not for his own life thy servant prays;
Love's dart in thy bent brows the Archer lays,
    Nor shoots in vain.

Art thou with grief afflicted, with the smart
    Of absence, and is bitter toil thy part?
Thy lamentations and thy tears, O Heart,
    Are not in vain!

Last night the wind from out her village blew,
And wandered all the garden alleys through,
O rose, tearing thy bosom's robe in two;
    'Twas not in vain!

And Hafiz, though thy heart within thee dies,
Hiding love's agony from curious eyes,
Ah, not in vain thy tears, not vain thy sighs,
    Not all in vain!

Vain to Seek the Key to the Hidden (5)

O Turkish maid of Shiraz! in thy hand
If thou'lt take my heart, for the mole on thy cheek
I would barter Bokhara and Samarkand.
Bring, Cup-bearer, all that is left of thy wine!
In the Garden of Paradise vainly thou'lt seek
The lip of the fountain of Ruknabad,
And the bowers of Mosalla where roses twine.

They have filled the city with blood and broil,
Those soft-voiced Lulis for whom we sigh;
As Turkish robbers fall on the spoil,
They have robbed and plundered the peace of my
        heart.
Dowered is my mistress, a beggar am I;
What shall I bring her? a beautiful face
Needs nor jewel nor mole nor the tiring-maid's art.

Brave tales of singers and wine relate,
The key to the Hidden 'twer vain to seek;
No wisdom of ours has unlocked that gate,
And locked to our wisdom it still shall be.
But of Joseph's beauty the lute shall speak;
And the minstrel knows that Zuleika came forth,
Love parting the curtains of modesty.

When thou spokest ill of thy servant 'twas well—
God pardon thee! for thy words were sweet;
Not unwelcomed the bitterest answer fell
From lips where the ruby and sugar lay.
But, fair Love, let good counsel direct thy feet;
Far dearer to youth than dear life itself
Are the warnings of one grown wise—and gray!

The song is sung and the pearl is strung;
Come hither, O Hafiz, and sing again!
And the listening Heavens above thee hung
Shall loose o'er thy verse the Pleiades' chain.

No Lover of Hypocrisy (6)

A flower-tinted cheek, the flowery close
Of the fair earth, these are enough for me—
Enough that in the meadow wanes and grows
The shadow of a graceful cypress-tree.
I am no lover of hypocrisy;
Of all the treasures that the earth can boast,
A brimming cup of wine I prize the most—
    This is enough for me!

To them that here renowned for virtue live,
A heavenly palace is the meet reward;
To me, the drunkard and the beggar, give
The temple of the grape with red wine stored!
Beside a river seat thee on the sward;
It floweth past—so flows thy life away,
So sweetly, swiftly, fleets our little day—
    Swift, but enough for me!

Look upon all the gold in the world's mart,
On all the tears the world hath shed in vain;
Shall they not satisfy thy craving heart?
I have enough of loss, enough of gain;
I have my Love, what more can I obtain?
Mine is the joy of her companionship
Whose healing lip is laid upon my lip—
    This is enough for me!

I pray thee send not forth my naked soul
From its poor house to seek for Paradise;
Though heaven and earth before me God unroll
Back to thy village still my spirit flies.
And, Hafiz, at the door of Kismet lies
No just complaint—a mind like water clear,
A song that swells and dies upon the ear,
    These are enough for thee!

Wine for a Thirsty World (8)

The rose has flushed red, the bud has burst,
And drunk with joy is the nightingale—
Hail, Sufis! lovers of wine, all hail!
For wine is proclaimed to a world athirst.
Like a rock your repentance seemed to you;
Behold the marvel! of what avail
Was your rock, for a goblet has cleft it in two!

Bring wine for the king and the slave at the gate!
Alike for all is the banquet spread,
And drunk and sober are warmed and fed.
When the feast is done and the night grows late,
And the second door of the tavern gapes wide,
The low and the mighty must bow the head
'Neath the archway of Life, to meet what ... outside?

Except thy road through affliction pass,
None may reach the halting-station of mirth;
God's treaty: Am I not Lord of the earth?
Man sealed with a sigh: Ah yes, alas!
Nor with Is nor Is Not let thy mind contend;
Rest assured all perfection of mortal birth
In the great Is Not at the last shall end.

For Assaf's pomp, and the steeds of the wind,
And the speech of birds, down the wind have fled,
And he that was lord of them all is dead
Of his mastery nothing remains behind.
Shoot not thy feathered arrow astray!
A bow-shot's length through the air it has sped,
And then ... dropped down in the dusty way.

But to thee, O Hafiz, to thee, O Tongue
That speaks through the mouth of the slender reed,
What thanks to thee when thy verses speed
From lip to lip, and the song thou hast sung?

Love-Drunk We Inherit Paradise (18)

Slaves of thy shining eyes are even those
That diadems of might and empire bear;
Drunk with the wine that from thy red lip flows,
Are they that e'en the grape's delight forswear.
Drift, like the wind across a violet bed,
Before thy many lovers, weeping low,
And clad like violets in blue robes of woe,
Who feel thy wind-blown hair and bow the head.

Thy messenger the breath of dawn, and mine
A stream of tears, since lover and beloved
Keep not their secret; through my verses shine,
Though other lays my flower's grace have proved
And countless nightingales have sung thy praise.
When veiled beneath thy curls thou passest, see,
To right and leftward those that welcome thee
Have bartered peace and rest on thee to gaze!

But thou that knowest God by heart, away!
Wine-drunk, love-drunk, we inherit Paradise,
His mercy is for sinners; hence and pray
Where wine thy cheek red as red erghwan dyes,
And leave the cell to faces sinister.
O Khizr, whose happy feet bathed in life's fount,
Help one who toils afoot—the horsemen mount
And hasten on their way; I scarce can stir.

Ah, loose me not! ah, set not Hafiz free
From out the bondage of thy gleaming hair!
Safe only those, safe, and at liberty,
That fast enchained in thy linked ringlets are.
But from the image of his dusty cheek
Learn this from Hafiz: proudest heads shall bend,
And dwellers on the threshold of a friend
Be crowned with the dust that crowns the meek.

Hafiz's Melody Consoles Weary Hearts (20)

From out the street of So-and-So,
O wind, bring perfumes sweet to me
For I am sick and pale with woe;
Oh bring me rest from misery!
The dust that lies before her door,
Love's long desired elixir, pour
Upon this wasted heart of mine—
Bring me a promise and a sign!

Between the ambush of mine eyes
And my heart's fort there's enmity—
Her eyebrow's bow, the dart that flies,
Beneath her lashes, bring to me!
Sorrow and absence, glances cold,
Before my time have made me old;
A wine-cup from the hand of Youth
Bring me for pity and for truth!

Then shall all unbelievers taste
A draft or two of that same wine;
But if they like it not, oh haste!
And let joy's flowing cup be mine.
Cup-bearer, seize today, nor wait
Until tomorrow!—or from Fate
Some passport to felicity,
Some written surety bring to me!

My heart threw back the veil of woe,
Consoled by Hafiz's melody:
From out the street of So-and-So,
O wind, bring perfumes sweet to me!

What Pain Is Worth (21)

Not all the sum of earthly happiness
Is worth the bowed head of a moment's pain,
And if I sell for wine my dervish dress,
Worth more than what I sell is what I gain!
Land where my Lady dwells, thou holdest me
Enchained; else Fars were but a barren soil,
Not worth the journey over land and sea,
    Not worth the toil!

Down in the quarter where they sell red wine,
My holy carpet scarce would fetch a cup—
How brave a pledge of piety is mine,
Which is not worth a gob let foaming up!
Mine enemy heaped scorn on me and said:
"Forth from the tavern gate!" Why am I thrust
From off the threshold? is my fallen head
    Not worth the dust?

Wash white that travel-stained sad robe of thine!
Where word and deed alike one color bear,
The grape's fair purple garment shall outshine
Thy many-colored rags and tattered gear.
Full easy seemed the sorrow of the sea
Lightened by hope of gain—hope flew too fast!
A hundred pearls were poor indemnity,
    Not worth the blast.

The sultan's crown, with priceless jewels set,
Encircles fear of death and constant dread;
It is a head-dress much desired—and yet
Art sure 'tis worth the danger to the head?
'Twere best for thee to hide thy face from those
That long for thee; the Conqueror's reward
Is never worth the army's long-drawn woes,
　　Worth fire and sword.

Ah, seek the treasure of a mind at rest
And store it in the treasury of Ease;
Not worth a loyal heart, a tranquil breast,
Were all the riches of thy lands and seas!
Ah, scorn, like Hafiz, the delights of earth,
Ask not one grain of favor from the base,
Two hundred sacks of jewels were not worth
　　Thy soul's disgrace!

Kisses Sweet (22)

The rose is not fair without the beloved's face,
Nor merry the Spring without the sweet laughter of
      wine;
The path through the fields, and winds from a
      flower-strewn place,
Without her bright cheek, which glows like a tulip fine,
Nor winds softly blowing, fields deep in corn, are fair.

And lips like to sugar, grace like a flower that sways,
Are nought without kisses many and dalliance sweet;
If thousands of voices sang not the rose's praise,
The joy of the cypress her opening bud to greet,
Nor dancing of boughs nor blossoming rose were fair.

Though limned by most skilful fingers, no pictures
      please
Unless the beloved's image is drawn therein;
The garden and flowers, and hair flowing loose on the
      breeze,
Unless to my Lady's side I may strive and win,
Nor garden, nor flowers, nor loose flying curls are fair.

Hast seen at a marriage-feast, when the mirth runs
      high,
The revelers scatter gold with a careless hand?
The gold of thy heart, O Hafiz, despised doth lie,
Not worthy thy love to be cast by a drunken band
At the feet of her who is fairer than all that's fair.

Dear Days That Perished
with My Friend (23)

My lady, that did change this house of mine,
Into a heaven when that she dwelt therein,
From head to foot an angel's grace divine
Entrapped her; pure she was, spotless of sin;
Fair as the moon her countenance, and wise;
Lords of the kind and tender glance, her eyes
With an abounding loveliness did shine.

Then said my heart: Here will I take my rest!
This city breathes her love in every part.
But to a distant bourn was she addressed,
Alas! he knew it not, alas, poor heart!
The influence of some cold malignant star
Has loosed my hand that held her, lone and far
She journeyed that lay upon my breast.

Not only did she lift my bosom's veil,
Reveal its inmost secret, but her grace
Drew back the curtain from Heaven's mansions pale,
And gave her there an eternal dwelling-place.
The flower-strewn river lip and meadows fair,
The rose herself but fleeting treasures were,
Regret and Winter follow in their trail.

Dear were the days which perished with my friend—
Ah, what is left of life, now she is dead,
All wisdomless and profitless I spend!
The nightingale his own life's blood doth shed,
When, to the kisses of the wind, the morn
Unveils the rose's splendor—with his torn
And jealous breast he dyes her petals red.

Yet pardon her, O Heart, for poor wert thou,
A humble dervish on the dusty way;
Crowned with the crown of empire was her brow,
And in the realms of beauty she bore sway.
But all the joy that Hafiz's hand might hold,
Lay in the beads that morn and eve he told,
Worn with God's praise; and see! he holds it now.

Where True Spiritual Passion Lies (24)

Not one is filled with madness like to mine
In all the taverns! My soiled robe lies here,
There my neglected book, both pledged for wine.
With dust my heart is thick, that should be clear,
A glass to mirror forth the Great King's face;
One ray of light from out Thy dwelling-place
To pierce my night, O God! and draw me near.

From out mine eyes unto my garment's hem
A river flows; perchance my cypress-tree
Beside that stream may rear her lofty stem,
Watering her roots with tears. Ah, bring to me
The wine vessel! Since my Love's cheek is hid,
A flood of grief comes from my heart unbid,
And turns mine eyes into a bitter sea!

Nay, by the hand that sells me wine, I vow
No more the brimming cup shall touch my lips,
Until my mistress with her radiant brow
Adorns my feast—until love's secret slips
From her, as from the candle's tongue of flame,
Though I, the singed moth, for very shame,
Dare not extol Love's light without eclipse.

Red wine I worship, and I worship her!—
Speak not to me of anything beside,
For nought but these on earth or heaven I care.
What though the proud narcissus flowers defied
Thy shining eyes to prove themselves more bright,
Yet heed them not! those that are clear of sight
Follow not them to whom all light's denied.

Before the tavern door a Christian sang
To sound of pipe and drum, what time the earth
Awaited the white dawn, and gaily rang
Upon mine ear those harbingers of mirth:
"If the True Faith be such as thou dost say,
Alas! my Hafiz, that this sweet To-day
Should bring unknown To-morrow to the birth!"

Praise for the End of Care (25)

The days of absence and the bitter nights
Of separation, all are at an end!
Where is the influence of the star that blights
My hope? The omen answers: At an end!
Autumn's abundance, creeping Autumn's mirth,
Are ended and forgot when o'er the earth
The wind of Spring with soft warm feet doth wend.

The Day of Hope, hid beneath Sorrow's veil,
Has shown its face—ah, cry that all may hear:
Come forth! the powers of night no more prevail!
Praise be to God, now that the rose is near
With long-desired arid flaming coronet,
The cruel stinging thorns all men forget,
The wind of Winter ends its proud career.

The long confusion of the nights that were,
Anguish that dwelt within my heart, is o'er;
'Neath the protection of my lady's hair
Grief nor disquiet come to me no more.
What though her curls wrought all my misery,
My lady's gracious face can comfort me,
And at the end give what I sorrow for.

Light-hearted to the tavern let me go,
Where laughs the pipe, the merry cymbals kiss;
Under the history of all my woe,
My mistress sets her hand and writes: Finis.
Oh, linger not, nor trust the inconstant days
That promised: Where thou art thy lady stays—
The tale of separation ends with this!

Joy's certain path, O Saki, thou hast shown—
Long may thy cup be full, thy days be fair!
Trouble and sickness from my breast have flown,
Order and health thy wisdom marshals there.
Not one that numbered Hafiz's name among
The great—unnumbered were his tears, unsung;
Praise him that sets an end to endless care!

Who Knows What Will? (26)

The secret draft of wine and love repressed
Are joys foundationless—then come whate'er
May come, slave to the grape I stand confessed!
Unloose, O friend, the knot of thy heart's care,
Despite the warning that the Heavens reveal!
For all his thought, never astronomer
That loosed the knot of Fate those Heavens conceal!

Not all the changes that thy days unfold
Shall rouse thy wonder; Time's revolving sphere
Over a thousand lives like thine has rolled.
That cup within thy fingers, dost not hear
The voices of dead kings speak through the clay
Kobad, Bahman, Djemshid, their dust is here,
"Gently upon me set thy lips!" they say.

What man can tell where Kaus and Kai have gone?
Who knows where even now the restless wind
Scatters the dust of Djem's imperial throne?
And where the tulip, following close behind
The feet of Spring, her scarlet chalice rears,
There Ferhad for the love of Shirin pined,
Dyeing the desert red with his heart's tears.

Bring, bring the cup! drink we while yet we may
To our soul's ruin the forbidden draft;
Perhaps a treasure-trove is hid away
Among those ruins where the wine has laughed!—
Perhaps the tulip knows the fickleness
Of Fortune's smile, for on her stalk's green shaft
She bears a wine-cup through the wilderness.

The murmuring stream of Ruknabad, the breeze
That blows from out Mosalla's fair pleasance,
Summon me back when I would seek heart's ease,
Traveling afar; what though Love's countenance
Be turned full harsh and sorrowful on me,
I care not so that Time's unfriendly glance
Still from my Lady's beauty turned be.

Like Hafiz, drain the goblet cheerfully
While minstrels touch the lute and sweetly sing,
For all that makes thy heart rejoice in thee
Hangs of Life's single, slender, silken string.

The Heart Is a Sea of Sorrow (27)

My friend has fled! alas, my friend has fled,
And left me nought but tears and pain behind!
Like smoke above a flame caught by the wind,
So rose she from my breast and forth she sped.
Drunk with desire, I seized Love's cup divine,
But she that held it poured the bitter wine
Of Separation into it and fled.

The hunter she, and I the helpless prey;
Wounded and sick, round me her toils she drew,
My heart into a sea of sorrow threw,
Bound up her camel loads and fled away.
Fain had I laid an ambush for her soul,
She saw and vanished, and the timid foal,
Good Fortune, slipped the rein and would not stay.

My heart was all too narrow for my woe,
And tears of blood my weeping eyes have shed,
A crimson stream across the desert sped,
Rising from out my sad heart's overflow.
She knew not what Love's meanest slave can tell:
"'Tis sweet to serve!" but threw me a Farewell,
Kissing my threshold, turned, and cried "I go!"

In the clear dawn, before the east was red,
Before the rose had torn her veil in two,
A nightingale through Hafiz's garden flew,
Stayed but to fill its song with tears, and fled.

Hidden Love's Wisdom (28)

Hast thou forgotten when thy stolen glance
Was turned to me, when on my happy face
Clearly thy love was writ, which doth enhance
All happiness? or when my sore disgrace
(Hast thou forgot?) drew from thine eyes reproof,
And made thee hold thy sweet red lips aloof,
Dowered, like Jesus' breath, with healing grace?

Hast thou forgotten how the glorious
Swift nights flew past, the cup of dawn brimmed high?
My love and I alone, God favoring us!
And when she like a waning moon did lie,
And Sleep had drawn his coif about her brow,
Hast thou forgot? Heaven's crescent moon would bow
The head, and in her service pace the sky!

Hast thou forgotten when, a sojourner
Within the tavern gates and drunk with wine,
I found Love's passionate wisdom hidden there,
Which in the mosque none even now divine?
The goblet's carbuncle (hast thou forgot?)
Laughed out aloud, and speech flew hot
And fast between thy ruby lips and mine!

Hast thou forgotten when thy cheek's dear torch
Lighted the beacon of desire in me,
And when my heart, like foolish moths that scorch
Their wings and yet return, turned all to thee?
Within the banquet-hall of Good Repute
(Hast thou forgot?) the wine's self-pressed my suit,
And filled the morn with drunken jollity!

Hast thou forgotten when thou laid'st aright
The uncut gems of Hafiz's inmost thought,
And side by side thy sweet care strung the bright
Array of verse on verse—hast thou forgot?

Like Dark Mines
Where Rubies Are Hidden (33)

The jewel of the secret treasury
Is still the same as once it was; the seal
Upon Love's treasure casket, and the key,
Are still what thieves can neither break nor steal;
Still among lovers loyalty is found,
And therefore faithful eyes still strew the ground
With the same pearls that mine once strewed for thee.

Question the wandering winds and thou shalt know
That from the dusk until the dawn doth break,
My consolation is that still they blow
The perfume of thy curls across my cheek.
A dart from thy bent brows has wounded me—
Ah, come! my heart still waiteth helplessly,
Has waited ever, till thou heal its pain.

If seekers after rubies there were none,
Still to the dark mines where the gems had lain
Would pierce, as he was wont, the radiant sun,
Setting the stones ablaze. Would'st hide the stain
Of my heart's blood? Blood-red the ruby glows
(And whence it came my wounded bosom knows)
Upon thy lips to show what thou hast done.

Let not thy curls waylay my pilgrim soul,
As robbers use, and plunder me no more!
Years join dead year, but thine extortionate rule
Is still the same, merciless as before.
Sing, Hafiz, sing again of eyes that weep!
For still the fountain of our tears is deep
As once it was, and still with tears is full.

Radiance Draws the Moth's Desire (34)

Last night I dreamed that angels stood without
The tavern door, and knocked in vain, and wept;
They took the clay of Adam, and, methought,
Molded a cup therewith while all men slept.
O dwellers in the halls of Chastity!
You brought Love's passionate red wine to me,
Down to the dust I am, your bright feet stepped.

For Heaven's self was all too weak, to bear
The burden of His love God laid on it,
He turned to seek a messenger elsewhere,
And in the Book of Fate my name was writ.
Between my Lord and me such concord lies
As makes the Huris glad in Paradise,
With songs of praise through the green glades they flit.

A hundred dreams of Fancy's garnered store
Assail me—Father Adam went astray
Tempted by one poor grain of corn! Wherefore
Absolve and pardon him that turns away
Though the soft breath of Truth reaches his ears,
For two-and-seventy jangling creeds he hears,
And loud-voiced Fable calls him ceaselessly.

That, that is not the flame of Love's true fire
Which makes the torchlight shadows dance in rings,
But where the radiance draws the moth's desire
And send him forth with scorched and drooping
        wings.
The heart of one who dwells retired shall break,
Rememb'ring a black mole and a red cheek,
And his life ebb, sapped at its secret springs.

Yet since the earliest time that man has sought
To comb the locks of Speech, his goodly bride,
Not one, like Hafiz, from the face of Thought
Has torn the veil of Ignorance aside.

Forget Nothing (35)

Forget not when dear friend to friend returned,
Forget not days gone by, forget them not!
My mouth has tasted bitterness, and learned
To drink the envenomed cup of mortal lot;
Forget not when a sweeter draft was mine,
Loud rose the songs of them that drank that wine—
    Forget them not!

Forget not loyal lovers long since dead,
Though faith and loyalty should be forgot,
Though the earth cover the enamored head,
And in the dust wisdom and passion rot.
My friends have thrust me from their memory;
Vainly a thousand thousand times I cry:
    Forget me not!

Weary I turn me to my bonds again.
Once there were hands strong to deliver me,
Forget not when they broke a poor slave's chain!
Though from mine eyes tears flow unceasingly,
I think on them whose rose gardens are set
Beside the Zindeh Rud, and I forget
    Life's misery.

Sorrow has made her lair in my breast,
And undisturbed she lies—forget them not
That drove her forth like to a hunted beast!
Hafiz, thou and thy tears shall be forgot,
Lock fast the gates of thy sad heart! But those
That held the key to thine unspoken woes—
    Forget them not!

Notes to the Poems

Throughout the excerpts of Gertrude Bell's original preface reprinted for this volume, we have updated spellings and grammar to be consistent with contemporary usage. This includes, for instance, Qur'an for Koran, Muhammad for Mahommad, Muslim for Muhammadan, where for whence, and humanity for man, when the latter was used to indicate both men and women.

The following notes to the poems were also written by Gertrude Bell.

Fresh and New (10)

This song is not to be found in the best editions of the *Divan* and is believed to be spurious; but it is printed in most of the popular editions, and is as widely known as any of the poems which pass with a better right under the name of Hafiz. It is set to a soft and well-nigh tuneless air which sounds like dream music, or the echo of something very beautiful coming from a great distance, the singer ending on an almost whispered repetition of the first exquisite phrase. I have been told that the boatmen on the Ganges sing it as they row, and the monotonous accompaniment of the water under the oars must be even more fitting to the melody than that of the lute strings.

Hafiz Can Lose No More (14)

Stanza 1: Hafiz wrote this poem upon the death of his son.

Stanza 3: Rosenzweig, in his edition of the *Divan,* says that the allusion is to the dust and water which God kneaded into the body of Adam, and that, out of derision, Hafiz calls the human body a house of joy. The moon, according to Persian superstition, has a baneful influence upon human life. Rosenzweig also remarks that "I had not castled" means that Hafiz had not taken the precaution of marrying his son, and so securing for himself grandchildren who would have been a consolation to him on their father's death. For that reason he had nothing more to lose, and was indifferent as to what his next move in the game should be.

The Glow of My Love's Red Cheek (9)

Stanza 1: This poem is addressed to the vizier of Sultan Oweis of Baghdad, Hadji Kawameddin, who founded a college for Hafiz in Shiraz. With true Persian exaggeration, the poet must needs write to his patron much in the same terms in which a lover would write to his mistress; but his words, though they sound strangely to our ears, are nothing more than the Oriental way of saying, "Awake, my St. John!"

The mystical interpretation of the first few lines is said to be: As the wine glows in the cup like the reflection of a ruddy cheek, so in the goblet of my heart I have seen the reflection of God, the true Beloved.

No Reproach for the Drunkard (17)

Stanza 3: The allusion is to the expulsion of Adam from the Garden of Eden.

Stanza 4: Concerning the last judgment, a beautiful tradition relates that there are seven degrees of punishment, but eight of blessedness, because God's mercy exceeds his justice.

Love at Least Exists (16)

Sidreh and Tuba are two trees in the Garden of Paradise. The former is the abode of the angel Gabriel. Concerning the latter, Sale says in *Introduction to the Koran:* "They fable that it stands in the palace of Muhammad, though a branch of it will reach to the house of every true believer; that it will be laden with pomegranates, grapes, dates, and other fruits of surprising bigness, and of tastes unknown to mortals. So that if a man desire to eat of any particular kind of fruit, it will immediately be presented to him; or if he choose flesh, birds ready dressed will be set before him, according to his wish. They add that the boughs of this tree will spontaneously bend down to the hand of the person who would gather of its fruits, and that it will supply the blessed not only with food, but also with silken garments and beasts to ride on, ready saddled and bridled

and adorned with rich trappings, which will burst forth
from its fruits; and that this tree is so large that a person
mounted on the fleetest horse would not be able to gallop
from one end of its shade to the other in a hundred
years."

Love Less Easy (1)

Stanza 1: The first line of this song is borrowed from an
Arabic poem by Yezid ibn Moawiyah, the second caliph
of the Ommiad line. This prince was held in abomina-
tion by the Persian Shi'ites, both as the head of the Sunnis
and because he was the cause of the death of Hussein, the
son of Ali, whom the Shi'ites regarded as the rightful
successor to the caliphate. Hafiz was frequently
reproached for setting a quotation from the works of the
abhorred Yezid at the head of his book—a reproach
which he is said to have met with the reply that it was
good policy to steal from the heretics whatsoever they
possessed of worth.

Whispered Prayers (3)

Stanza 1: King Solomon sent the lapwing, or hoopoe, as
his messenger to Bilkis, Queen of Sheba. The story is told
thus by Al Ta'labi, in his *Stories of the Prophets.* (The lap-
wing had already made a journey on his own account,
and had brought not a worshiper of the true God.) "Then
Solomon wrote a letter saying: From the servant of God,
Solomon, son of David, to Bilkis, Queen of Saba, in the

name of God the Merciful, the Compassionate, peace be upon him who follows the right road. After which he said: Behave not insolently toward me, but come unto me humbled; and he sealed it with his seal. Then he said to the lapwing: Fly with this letter and deliver it unto them, then turn away, but remain near them and hear what answer they make. And the lapwing took the letter and flew with it to Bilkis. And she was in the land which is called Marib, at a distance of three days' journey, and she had entered into her castle, and the gates of it were shut. For when she slept she was wont to shut the gates and to take the key and lay it beneath her head. So the lapwing came unto her, and she was asleep, lying upon her back; and he laid the letter upon her breast. Wahb ibn Manabbih says that there was a window opposite to the sun so that the sunbeams fell through it at dawn, and when she saw the sun she was wont to bow down and worship it. And the lapwing went to this window and blocked it up with his wings. And the sun rose, but she knew it not. And she thought that the sun was late, and stood up to look for it. Then the lapwing threw a leaf upon her face. And they say that Bilkis took the letter and she was able to read the writing. But when she saw the seal she trembled and bowed down, because of the power of Solomon that was in his seal. For she knew that the power of him who had sent the letter was greater than hers, and she said: Lo, here is a king whose messengers are the birds; verily he is a mighty king."

Stanzas 5 and 6: The accepted explanation of these lines is that by the glass Hafiz means his own heart, which he sends to his mistress that she may see that her own image is reflected in it; but I prefer here (and indeed for the whole poem) a mystical interpretation. The heavenly voice tells him to seek for comfort in Sufism, and bids him look upon the mirror, for he shall see God himself reflected in it—which is only another way of putting the doctrine that humanity and God are one.

Vain to Seek the Key to the Hidden (5)

Stanza 1: When the conqueror Timur entered Shiraz, it is related that he summoned Hafiz before him and said: "Of all my empire, Bokhara and Samarkand are the fairest jewels; how comes it that in thy song thou hast declared that thou would'st exchange them against the black mole on the cheek of thy mistress?" Hafiz replied: "It is because of such generosity that I am now as poor as thou seest." The Emperor was not to be outdone in repartee: he sent the poet away a richer man by some hundreds of gold pieces.

In the garden of Mosalla, Hafiz lies buried; the stream Ruknabad flows near at hand.

Stanza 3: Joseph is the Oriental archetype of perfect beauty. The story of his relations with Zuleika, Potiphar's wife, is one of the famous love stories of the East; Jāmī made it the theme of a long metaphysical poem.

The whole poem has received a mystical interpretation which seems to me to add but little to its value or to its intelligibility; but in case anyone should wish to gather the higher wisdom from it, I may mention that the mole, powder, and paint, of which a beautiful face does not stand in need, represent the ink, color, dots, and lines of the Qur'an; and this is the explanation given to the couplet concerning Joseph and Zuleika by a thorough-going Western mystic: "By reason of that beauty daily increasing that Joseph the absolute existence, the real beloved, God had, I the first day knew that love for him would bring Zuleikha us, things possible forth from the screen of chastity the pure existence of God." The learned translator seems to have felt that his version presented some difficulties, and he adds for the use of his weaker brethren the following comment: "In the world of nonexistence and possibility, when I beheld the splendor of true beauty with different qualities, I knew for certain that Love would take us out of the ambush." This makes everything clear!

Wine for a Thirsty World (8)

Stanza 3: When God had created human beings and made them wiser than the angels, he bound them to himself by a solemn treaty. "Am I not thy Lord who has created thee?" he demanded, and they answered "Yes." But the Arabic word *bala,* which signifies "assent," means also "sorrow," and they say that the first of our fathers knew full well what a terrible gift was that life which he had received from his Lord, and sealed the treaty with a seal of grief. Therefore, since the earliest day, life and sorrow have gone hand in hand, bound together by the first great pact between God and humanity.

Solomon, the archetype of human greatness, is the king whose mastery has left nothing behind. He harnessed the wind as a steed to his chariot, he spoke with the birds in their own tongue, and the wise and magnificent Assaf was his minister. Upon his seal was engraved the name of God, which is unknown to humans and before which the Jinn and the Angels must bow down. It was with this seal that he fastened up the bottles in which he imprisoned the Jinn—those bottles which the fishermen in the *Arabian Nights* pull up in their nets.

Love-Drunk We Inherit Paradise (18)

Stanza 1: Blue is the Persian color of mourning. Hafiz compares the weeping lovers, clad in robes of grief, to a bed of violets, and as the violets bow their heads when the wind passed over them, so they bow down when their mistress passes by with flowing curls.

Stanza 3: Erghwan: the Syringa Persica, or Persian lilac. In the early spring, before it comes into leaf, it is covered with buds of a beautiful reddish-purple color. Khizr: a prophet whom Muslims confound with Phineas, Ellas, and St. George, saying that his soul passed by metempsychosis successively through all three. He discovered the fountain of life and drank of it, thereby making himself immortal. It is said that he guided Alexander to the same fountain, which lay in the Land of Darkness. It was he, too, for whom Moses set out to seek when he had been informed by God that Al Khizr was wiser than he. He found him seated on a rock, at the meeting of the two seas, and followed him for a time, learning wisdom from him, as is related in the eighteenth chapter of the Quran. His name means "green"; wherever his feet rested, the earth was covered with green herbs.

Hafiz looked upon the prophet Al Khizr as one of his special guardians. About four Persian miles from Shiraz there is a spot called Pir-i-Sabz, the Old Green Man; whosoever should pass forty nights in it without sleeping, on the fortieth night Al Khizr would appear to him and confer upon him the immortal gift of song. Hafiz in his youth fell in love with a beautiful girl of Shiraz called Shakh-i-Nahat, and in order to win her heart he determined to meet Al Khizr and receive from him the art of poetry. For thirty-nine mornings he walked beneath the windows of Shakh-i-Nahat, at noon he ate, then he slept, and at night he kept watch, undismayed by the terrible apparition of a fierce lion which was his nightly companion. At length, on the fortieth morning, Shakh-i-Nahat called him into her house and told him that she was ready to become his wife, for she preferred a man of genius to the son of a king. She would have kept him with her, but Hafiz, though he had gained his original end, was now filled with desire to become a poet, and insisted upon keeping his fortieth vigil. That night an old man dressed in green garments came to him and brought him a cup of the water of immortality.

What Pain Is Worth *(21)*

Stanza 2: The prayer-carpet of the orthodox Muslim had not enough value to procure for him so much as one glass of Sufi wine. Nor was he worthy to lay his head even upon the dusty steps of the tavern—the place of instruction.

Stanza 3: To be clothed in one color is the Persian idiom for sincerity. He means that the single purple robe of the grape is worth more than the hypocritical garment of the dervish, all torn and patched with long journeying—in the wrong road.

Stanza 5: So far I have endeavored to give the mystical interpretation of the poem. There is, however, a story attached to it which turns it into a historical rather than a theological document. It is related that the king of the Deccan, Mahmud Shah Bahmani, had heard of the fame of Hafiz and, having a pretty taste in literature, was desirous of attracting him to his court. Accordingly he ordered his vizier, Mir Feiz Allah Inju, to send the poet a sufficient sum to pay for his journey from Shiraz. Hafiz resolved to accept the invitation. He wound up his affairs in his native town, using some of the money the sultan had sent him in paying his debts and in making gifts to his sister's children, and set forth upon his journey. But when he reached the town of Lar, he found there an acquaintance in very bad case, having been plundered by robbers and reduced to a state of beggary. Hafiz was moved to compassion and gave him the remainder of the money which Mahmud Shah had sent to him. He was now himself unable to continue his journey for want of means, and perhaps it was bitter experience that taught him that in very fact his prayer-carpet would not fetch him a glass of wine, and that without the necessary silver pieces he would be thrust from out the tavern doors. From these straits he was rescued by two friendly merchants, who were also on their way to India, and who offered to pay his expenses to Hormuz, and there place him on a vessel of Mahmud Shah's which was coming to fetch them. Hafiz accepted the offer, went to Hormuz, and embarked on the ship. But before they had left the port a violent storm arose, and persuaded the poet that no advantages he might reap from the journey would be worth the sorrow of the sea. Under pretext of bidding farewell to friends, he disembarked, and in all haste made the best of his way back to Shiraz sending to Feiz Allah this poem as an excuse for failing to keep his engagement. The vizier read it to Mahmud Shah, who was transported by the beauty of the verses and the philosophic dignity in which Hafiz had cloaked his fears of the dangers of the road and the discomforts of seasickness. With singular generosity, he sent the defaulting poet a further present, consisting of some at least of the riches of his lands and seas.

Dear Days That Perished with My Friend (23)

This poem is said to have been written by Hafiz upon the death of his wife.

Where True Spiritual Passion Lies (24)

Stanza 5: Shah Shudja, as has been related in the introduction, "Who is Hafiz?," was not always on the best of terms with Hafiz, partly because he was jealous of the latter's fame as a poet, and partly because Hafiz had been the protégé of Shah Shudja's former rival, Abu Ishac. Accordingly, the King looked about for some means of doing the poet an injury, nor was it long before he found what he sought. He accused Hafiz of denying the Resurrection, basing the accusation upon the last couplet of this poem—the last three lines of the present translation—and cited him before the Ulema as an infidel. But Hafiz was too many for him. Before the day on which he was to answer the charge against himself, he inserted another couplet into the ode, in which he stated that the dangerous lines did not express his own opinion but that of the heretical Christian. He came off with flying colors; for not only was he entirely cleared, but it was also acknowledged that he had dealt a good blow on behalf of Islam, since he had shown up one of the errors of the infidel.

Who Knows What Will? (26)

Stanza 3: The loves of Ferhad and Shirin are famous in Persian legend. Shirin is called by some Mary, and by others Irene. The Greeks describe her as a Roman by birth and a Christian; the Turks and the Persians say that she was a daughter of the Emperor Maurice, and wife of Khusro Parwiz, who came to the Persian throne in 591 C.E. It was Khusro Parwiz who conquered Jerusalem and carried off, say the Persians, the true Cross, which had been enclosed in a gold box and buried in the ground. He was devotedly attached to his wife, Shirin, but she had given her heart to her humble lover, Ferhad. He, despairing of ever reaching one whose rank had placed her so far above him, wandered through the deserts and the mountains of Persia calling upon her name, and in order to beguile his weary hours executed the sculptures upon the rock Behistun—so says the legend. At length the king sent to him and told him that if he would cut through the rock and cause a stream upon the other side of the mountains to flow through it, he would relinquish Shirin to him. Ferhad set himself to the task, and had almost accomplished it when Khusro sent him the false news of Shirin's death. On hearing it, Ferhad threw himself from the top of the rock and so died. Shirin's end was scarcely less tragic. Khusro Parwiz was put to a violent death by his son, who proceeded to make proposals of marriage to his father's widow. Shirin promised to marry him if he would allow her to see once more her husband's corpse. She was led to the place where the murdered king lay, and, drawing a dagger, she stabbed herself and fell dead across his body.

It is difficult to conceive anything more exquisite than the little scarlet tulip growing upon a barren Persian hillside. On the top of a bleak pass over the mountains between Resht and Tehran, I have seen companies of tiny tulips shining like jewels among the dust and stones.

There is a tradition that this poem was sent to the King of Golconda.

Hidden Love's Wisdom (28)

Stanza 1: According to Oriental belief, Jesus Christ's gift of healing was due to a miraculous quality in his breath.

Radiance Draws the Moth's Desire (34)

Stanza 1: The story of the creation of Adam, and of the part played in it by the angels, appears in the Qur'an, chapter 11.

Tradition has amplified and adorned the story. It is said that the three archangels, Gabriel, Michael, and Israfil, were each in turn ordered to take from the earth seven handfuls of clay of three different colors—red, white, and yellow—that God might create out of it the races of humankind. But each in turn was moved by the earth's prayer that he would not rob her of her substance, and each returned to heaven empty-handed. The fourth time God sent Azrail, the angel of death, who tore the seven handfuls from the earth but, hearing her lamentations, promised her that the human substance would return to the earth from whence it had been taken. With the clay that Azrail brought him, God molded the figure of man, and when it was finished he left it forty days to dry. The angels came often to gaze upon it, and Eblis, kicking it with his foot, found that it rang hollow. When the figure of clay was dry, God breathed the breath of life into its nostrils, and ordered the angels to submit to the man he had created. But Eblis refused, saying that he had been created of pure fire, and would not serve a hollow mold of clay; for which God cast him out of Paradise. The rest of the angels acknowledged the superiority of Adam after God had made him tell them the names of all the creatures of the earth, though they had at first protested that it was not seemly that they should bow down to him, for their love for God was greater than his.

It is with this legend in mind that Hafiz has the angels standing at the tavern door where humanity may enter to receive instruction in God's wisdom, but where the angels must knock in vain. The angels also mold a wine-cup with the despised clay out of which the human body was molded, by which I think Hafiz means that a human being is the vessel into which divine love and wisdom are poured. When Hafiz says that the angels first brought him wine, he means that by their example they showed him what it was to be intoxicated by the contemplation of God.

Stanza 3: There are supposed to be seventy-two sects in Islam. Many Muslim writers compare them to the seventy-two branches of the family of Noah after the Babylonian confusion of tongues and the dispersal of the children of Adam.

Notes

Preface

1. All translations from Persian and Arabic in the preface are by Ibrahim Gamard. Italics indicate words added for clarity of meaning. The Qur'an is abbreviated as Q.
2. Annemarie Schimmel, *Mystical Dimensions of Islam* (Chapel Hill: University of North Carolina Press, 1975), 309.

Hafiz's Personal History

1. The phrase "vicar of Bray" comes from an old English song, describing a character who always switches sides, allying himself with whichever new government has come into power.

A Short Introduction to Hafiz's Mysticism

1. Martin Lings, *A Sufi Saint of the Twentieth Century: Shaiḳ Ahmad Al-'Alawī, His Spiritual Heritage and Legacy,* 2nd ed. (Berkeley: University of California Press, 1973), 34, note 1.
2. Laleh Bakhtiar, *Sufi: Expressions of the Mystic Quest* (London: Thames and Hudson, 1997), 9.
3. Hazrat Inayat Khan, *Complete Works of Pir-o-Murshid Inayat Khan, Sayings I,* ed. Munira van Voorst van Beest (London: East-West Publications, 1989), 346.

4. Al-Hakim Al-Tirhidhi, "A Treatise on the Heart," trans. Nicholas Heer, in *Three Early Sufi Texts* (Louisville, Ky.: Fons Vitae, 2003), 23.

The Poems

1. Laleh Bakhtiar, *Sufi,* 9.
2. Idries Shah, "Introduction to Teachings of Hafiz," in *Teachings of Hafiz: Selections from the Diwan,* trans. Gertrude Bell (London: Octagon Press, 1979), 9.
3. Daniel Ladinsky, *The Gift: Poems by Hafiz the Great Sufi Master* (New York: Penguin/Arkana, 1999), 2.
4. Bakhtiar, *Sufi,* 113.
5. Ibid.

About the Translator

Gertrude Bell (1868–1926) was an adventurer, scholar, linguist, and British intelligence officer. Misunderstood by many of her Victorian contemporaries, as was Richard Francis Burton, to whom she is often compared, Bell's courageous travels in the Islamic world of the Middle East in the late nineteenth century offered some of the first Western understandings of the culture and people of the lands of modern-day Iraq and Iran. Her translations of the poems of Hafiz are still considered by many scholars to be the most faithful of any in the English language. Her introduction to the poet, and notes on the poems themselves, were all written from firsthand research and experience in the lands and with the people who knew Hafiz's poetry most intimately.

Index of Poems *(by title)*

Index of First Lines

Other Books in
The Mystic Poets Series

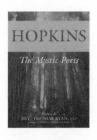

HOPKINS

Preface by
Rev. Thomas Ryan, CSP

TAGORE

Preface by
Swami Adiswaranda,
Minister and Spiritual Leader of
the Ramakrishna-Vivekananda
Center of New York; author of
Meditation & Its Practices

Forthcoming in the Series

HILDEGARD
WHITMAN

Notes

Notes

Notes

Notes

Notes

Notes

About SKYLIGHT PATHS Publishing

SkyLight Paths Publishing is creating a place where people of different spiritual traditions come together for challenge and inspiration, a place where we can help each other understand the mystery that lies at the heart of our existence.

Through spirituality, our religious beliefs are increasingly becoming a part of our lives—rather than *apart* from our lives. While many of us may be more interested than ever in spiritual growth, we may be less firmly planted in traditional religion. Yet, we to want to deepen our relationship to the sacred, to learn from our own as well as from other faith traditions, and to practice in new ways.

SkyLight Paths sees both believers and seekers as a community that increasingly transcends traditional boundaries of religion and denomination—people wanting to learn from each other, *walking together, finding the way.*

We at SkyLight Paths take great care to produce beautiful books that present meaningful spiritual content in a form that reflects the art of making high quality books. Therefore, we want to acknowledge those who contributed to the production of this book.

PRODUCTION
Tim Holtz and Bridgett Taylor

EDITORIAL
Sarah McBride, Maura Shaw & Emily Wichland

JACKET DESIGN
Bridgett Taylor

TEXT DESIGN
Bridgett Taylor

PRINTING & BINDING
Friesens Corporation, Manitoba, Canada

Other Interesting Books—Spirituality

Lighting the Lamp of Wisdom
A Week Inside an Ashram
by *John Ittner;* foreword by *Dr. David Frawley*

This insider's guide to Hindu spiritual life takes you into a typical week of retreat inside an ashram to demystify the ashram experience and show you what to expect from your own visit. Includes a discussion of worship services, meditation and yoga classes, chanting and music, work practice, and more.

6 x 9, 192 pp, b/w photographs, Quality PB, ISBN 1-893361-52-7 **$15.95**;
HC, ISBN 1-893361-37-3 **$24.95**

Waking Up
A Week Inside a Zen Monastery
by *Jack Maguire;* foreword by *John Daido Loori, Roshi*

An essential guide to what it's like to spend a week inside a Zen Buddhist monastery.

6 x 9, 224 pp, b/w photographs, Quality PB, ISBN 1-893361-55-1 **$16.95**;
HC, ISBN 1-893361-13-6 **$21.95**

Making a Heart for God
A Week Inside a Catholic Monastery
by *Dianne Aprile;* foreword by *Brother Patrick Hart,* OCSO

This essential guide to experiencing life in a Catholic monastery takes you to the Abbey of Gethsemani—the Trappist monastery in Kentucky that was home to author Thomas Merton—to explore the details. "More balanced and informative than the popular *The Cloister Walk* by Kathleen Norris." —*Choice: Current Reviews for Academic Libraries*

6 x 9, 224 pp, b/w photographs, Quality PB, ISBN 1-893361-49-7 **$16.95**;
HC, ISBN 1-893361-14-4 **$21.95**

Come and Sit
A Week Inside Meditation Centers
by *Marcia Z. Nelson;* foreword by *Wayne Teasdale*

The insider's guide to meditation in a variety of different spiritual traditions. Traveling through Buddhist, Hindu, Christian, Jewish, and Sufi traditions, this essential guide takes you to different meditation centers to meet the teachers and students and learn about the practices, demystifying the meditation experience.

6 x 9, 224 pp, b/w photographs, Quality PB, ISBN 1-893361-35-7 **$16.95**

Or phone, fax, mail, or e-mail to: SKYLIGHT PATHS Publishing
Sunset Farm Offices, Route 4 • P.O. Box 237 • Woodstock, Vermont 05091
Tel: (802) 457-4000   Fax: (802) 457-4004   www.skylightpaths.com
Credit card orders: (800) 962-4544 (8:30AM–5:30PM ET Monday–Friday)
Generous discounts on quantity orders. Satisfaction guaranteed. Prices subject to change.

Spiritual Practice

Finding Grace at the Center
The Beginning of Centering Prayer, 25th Anniversary Edition
by *M. Basil Pennington, OCSO, Thomas Keating, OCSO,* and *Thomas E. Clarke, SJ*

The book that helped launch the Centering Prayer "movement." Explains the prayer of *The Cloud of Unknowing,* posture and relaxation, the three simple rules of centering prayer, and how to cultivate centering prayer throughout all aspects of your life.

5 x 7¼, 112 pp, HC, ISBN 1-893361-69-1 **$14.95**

Three Gates to Meditation Practice
A Personal Journey into Sufism, Buddhism, and Judaism
by *David A. Cooper*

Shows us how practicing within more than one spiritual tradition can lead us to our true home.

Here are over fifteen years from the journey of "post-denominational rabbi" David A. Cooper, author of *God Is a Verb,* and his wife, Shoshana—years in which the Coopers explored a rich variety of practices, from chanting Sufi *dhikr* to Buddhist Vipassanā meditation, to the study of kabbalah and esoteric Judaism. Their experience demonstrates that the spiritual path is really completely within our reach, whoever we are, whatever we do—as long as we are willing to practice it.

5½ x 8½, 240 pp, Quality PB, ISBN 1-893361-22-5 **$16.95**

Praying with Our Hands: *Twenty-One Practices of Embodied Prayer from the World's Spiritual Traditions*
by *Jon M. Sweeney;* photographs by *Jennifer J. Wilson;*
foreword by *Mother Tessa Bielecki;* afterword by *Taitetsu Unno, Ph.D.*

A spiritual guidebook for bringing prayer into our bodies.

This inspiring book of reflections and accompanying photographs shows us twenty-one simple ways of using our hands to speak to God, to enrich our devotion and ritual. All express the various approaches of the world's religious traditions to bringing the body into worship. Spiritual traditions represented include Anglican, Sufi, Zen, Roman Catholic, Yoga, Shaker, Hindu, Jewish, Pentecostal, Eastern Orthodox, and many others.

8 x 8, 96 pp, 22 duotone photographs, Quality PB, ISBN 1-893361-16-0 **$16.95**

Labyrinths from the Outside In
Walking to Spiritual Insight—a Beginner's Guide
by *Donna Schaper* and *Carole Ann Camp*

The user-friendly, interfaith guide to making and using labyrinths—for meditation, prayer, and celebration.

Labyrinth walking is a spiritual exercise *anyone* can do. This accessible guide unlocks the mysteries of the labyrinth for all of us, providing ideas for using the labyrinth walk for prayer, meditation, and celebrations to mark the most important moments in life. Includes instructions for making a labyrinth of your own and finding one in your area.

6 x 9, 208 pp, b/w illus. and photographs, Quality PB, ISBN 1-893361-18-7 **$16.95**

Spiritual Biography

The Life of Evelyn Underhill
An Intimate Portrait of the Groundbreaking Author of Mysticism
by *Margaret Cropper;* foreword by *Dana Greene*

Evelyn Underhill was a passionate writer and teacher who wrote elegantly on mysticism, worship, and devotional life. This is the story of how she made her way toward spiritual maturity, from her early days of agnosticism to the years when her influence was felt throughout the world.

6 x 9, 288 pp, 5 b/w photos, Quality PB, ISBN 1-893361-70-5 **$18.95**

Zen Effects: *The Life of Alan Watts*
by *Monica Furlong*

The first and only full-length biography of one of the most charismatic spiritual leaders of the twentieth century—now back in print!

Through his widely popular books and lectures, Alan Watts (1915–1973) did more to introduce Eastern philosophy and religion to Western minds than any figure before or since. Here is the only biography of this charismatic figure, who served as Zen teacher, Anglican priest, lecturer, academic, entertainer, a leader of the San Francisco renaissance, and author of more than thirty books, including *The Way of Zen, Psychotherapy East and West* and *The Spirit of Zen.*

6 x 9, 264 pp, Quality PB, ISBN 1-893361-32-2 **$16.95**

Simone Weil: *A Modern Pilgrimage*
by *Robert Coles*

The extraordinary life of the spiritual philosopher who's been called both saint and madwoman.

The French writer and philosopher Simone Weil (1906–1943) devoted her life to a search for God—while avoiding membership in organized religion. Robert Coles' intriguing study of Weil details her short, eventful life, and is an insightful portrait of the beloved and controversial thinker whose life and writings influenced many (from T. S. Eliot to Adrienne Rich to Albert Camus), and continue to inspire seekers everywhere.

6 x 9, 208 pp, Quality PB, ISBN 1-893361-34-9 **$16.95**

Mahatma Gandhi: *His Life and Ideas*
by *Charles F. Andrews;* foreword by *Dr. Arun Gandhi*

An intimate biography of one of the greatest social and religious reformers of the modern world.

Examines from a contemporary Christian activist's point of view the religious ideas and political dynamics that influenced the birth of the peaceful resistance movement, the primary tool that Gandhi and the people of his homeland would use to gain India its freedom from British rule. An ideal introduction to the life and life's work of this great spiritual leader.

6 x 9, 336 pp, 5 b/w photos, Quality PB, ISBN 1-893361-89-6 **$18.95**

SkyLight Illuminations
Andrew Harvey, series editor

Offers today's spiritual seeker an enjoyable entry into the classic texts of the world's spiritual traditions. Each is presented in an accessible translation, with facing pages of guided commentary from experts, giving you the keys you need to understand the history, context, and meaning of the text. This series enables readers of all backgrounds to experience and understand classic spiritual texts directly, and to make them a part of their lives.

Dhammapada: *Annotated & Explained*
Translation by *Max Müller;* annotation by *Jack Maguire*

The most beloved of all the Buddhist scriptures.

The Dhammapada—words spoken by the Buddha himself over 2,500 years ago—is notoriously difficult to understand for the first-time reader. Now you can experience the Dhammapada with understanding even if you have no previous knowledge of Buddhism. Enlightening facing-page commentary explains all the names, terms and references, giving you deeper insight into the text. An excellent introduction to Buddhist life and practice.

5½ x 8½, 160 pp, Quality PB, ISBN 1-893361-42-X **$14.95**

Rumi and Islam—Selections from his Stories, Poems, and Discourses: *Annotated & Explained*
Translation and annotation by *Ibrahim Gamard*

Sheds new light on the religion of Rumi through a satisfying taste of Islamic Sufi mysticism.

Offers a new way of thinking about Rumi's poetry. Ibrahim Gamard focuses on Rumi's place within the Sufi tradition of Islam, providing readers with an image of the mystical side of the religion—one that has love of God at its core and sublime wisdom teachings as its pathways.

5½ x 8½, 240 pp, Quality PB, ISBN 1-59473-002-4 **$15.99**

Zohar: *Annotated & Explained*
Translation and annotation by *Daniel C. Matt*

The cornerstone text of Kabbalah, now with facing-page commentary that illuminates and explains the text for you.

The best-selling author of *The Essential Kabbalah* brings together in one place the most important teachings of the *Zohar,* the canonical text of Jewish mystical tradition. Guides readers step by step through the midrash, mystical fantasy and Hebrew scripture that make up the *Zohar,* explaining the inner meanings in facing-page commentary. Ideal for readers without any prior knowledge of Jewish mysticism.

5½ x 8½, 176 pp, Quality PB, ISBN 1-893361-51-9 **$15.99**

SkyLight Illuminations
Andrew Harvey, series editor

Selections from the Gospel of Sri Ramakrishna
Annotated & Explained
Translation by *Swami Nikhilananda;* annotation by *Kendra Crossen Burroughs*

The words of India's greatest example of God-consciousness and mystical ecstasy in recent history.

Introduces the fascinating world of the Indian mystic and the universal appeal of his message that has inspired millions of devotees for more than a century. Selections from the original text and insightful yet unobtrusive commentary highlight the most important and inspirational teachings. Ideal for readers without any prior knowledge of Hinduism.
5½ x 8½, 240 pp, b/w photographs, Quality PB, ISBN 1-893361-46-2 **$16.95**

Hasidic Tales: *Annotated & Explained*
Translation and annotation by *Rabbi Rami Shapiro*

The legendary tales of the impassioned Hasidic rabbis.

The allegorical quality of Hasidic tales can be perplexing. Here, they are presented as stories rather than parables, making them accessible and meaningful. Each demonstrates the spiritual power of unabashed joy, offers lessons for leading a holy life, and reminds us that the Divine can be found in the everyday. Annotations explain theological concepts, introduce major characters, and clarify references unfamiliar to most readers.
5½ x 8½, 240 pp, Quality PB, ISBN 1-893361-86-1 **$16.95**

The Way of a Pilgrim: *Annotated & Explained*
Translation and annotation by *Gleb Pokrovsky*

This delightful account is the story of one man who sets out to learn the prayer of the heart—also known as the "Jesus prayer"—and how the practice transforms his existence. This edition guides you through the text with facing-page annotations explaining names, terms, and references.
5½ x 8½, 160 pp, b/w illustrations, Quality PB, ISBN 1-893361-31-4 **$14.95**

Bhagavad Gita: *Annotated & Explained*
Translation by *Shri Purohit Swami;* annotation by *Kendra Crossen Burroughs*

"The very best Gita for first-time readers." —Ken Wilber

Millions of people turn daily to India's most beloved holy book, whose universal appeal has made it popular with non-Hindus and Hindus alike. This edition introduces readers to the characters; explains references and philosophical terms; shares the interpretations of famous spiritual leaders and scholars; and more.
5½ x 8½, 192 pp, Quality PB, ISBN 1-893361-28-4 **$16.95**

Spirituality

Bede Griffiths
An Introduction to His Interspiritual Thought
by *Wayne Teasdale*

The first in-depth study of Bede Griffiths' contemplative experience and thought.

Wayne Teasdale, a longtime personal friend and student of Griffiths, creates in this intimate portrait an intriguing view into the beliefs and life of this champion of interreligious acceptance and harmony. Explains key terms that form the basis of Griffiths' contemplative understanding, and the essential characteristics of his theology as they relate to the Hindu and Christian traditions.

6 x 9, 288 pp, Quality PB, ISBN 1-893361-77-2 **$18.95**

The Alphabet of Paradise: *An A–Z of Spirituality for Everyday Life*
by *Howard Cooper*

One of the most eloquent new voices in spirituality, Howard Cooper takes us on a journey of discovery—into ourselves and into the past—to find the signposts that can help us live more meaningful lives. In twenty-six engaging chapters—from A to Z—Cooper spiritually illuminates the subjects of daily life, using an ancient Jewish mystical method of interpretation that reveals both the literal and more allusive meanings of each. Topics include: Awe, Bodies, Creativity, Dreams, Emotions, Sports, and more.

5 x 7¾, 224 pp, Quality PB, ISBN 1-893361-80-2 **$16.95**

Winter: *A Spiritual Biography of the Season*
Edited by *Gary Schmidt* and *Susan M. Felch;* illustrations by *Barry Moser*

Explore how the dormancy of winter can be a time of spiritual preparation and transformation.

In thirty stirring pieces, *Winter* delves into the varied feelings that winter conjures in us, calling up both the barrenness and the beauty of the natural world in wintertime. Includes selections by Will Campbell, Rachel Carson, Annie Dillard, Donald Hall, Ron Hansen, Jane Kenyon, Jamaica Kincaid, Barry Lopez, Kathleen Norris, John Updike, E. B. White, and many others. "This outstanding anthology features top-flight nature and spirituality writers on the fierce, inexorable season of winter.... Remarkably lively and warm, despite the icy subject." —★*Publishers Weekly* Starred Review

6 x 9, 288 pp, 6 b/w illus., Quality PB, ISBN 1-893361-92-6 **$18.95**;
HC, ISBN 1-893361-53-5 **$21.95**

Religious Etiquette/Reference

How to Be a Perfect Stranger, 3rd Edition
The Essential Religious Etiquette Handbook
Edited by *Stuart M. Matlins* and *Arthur J. Magida*

The indispensable guidebook to help the well-meaning guest when visiting other people's religious ceremonies.

A straightforward guide to the rituals and celebrations of the major religions and denominations in the United States and Canada from the perspective of an interested guest of any other faith, based on information obtained from authorities of each religion. Belongs in every living room, library, and office.

COVERS:

African American Methodist Churches • Assemblies of God • Baha'i • Baptist • Buddhist • Christian Church (Disciples of Christ) • Christian Science (Church of Christ, Scientist) • Churches of Christ • Episcopalian and Anglican • Hindu • Islam • Jehovah's Witnesses • Jewish • Lutheran • Mennonite/Amish • Methodist • Mormon (Church of Jesus Christ of Latter-day Saints) • Native American/First Nations • Orthodox Churches • Pentecostal Church of God • Presbyterian • Quaker (Religious Society of Friends) • Reformed Church in America/Canada • Roman Catholic • Seventh-day Adventist • Sikh • Unitarian Universalist • United Church of Canada • United Church of Christ
6 x 9, 432 pp, Quality PB, ISBN 1-893361-67-5 **$19.95**

Also available:

The Perfect Stranger's Guide to Funerals and Grieving Practices
A Guide to Etiquette in Other People's Religious Ceremonies
Edited by *Stuart M. Matlins*
6 x 9, 240 pp, Quality PB, ISBN 1-893361-20-9 **$16.95**

The Perfect Stranger's Guide to Wedding Ceremonies
A Guide to Etiquette in Other People's Religious Ceremonies
Edited by *Stuart M. Matlins*
6 x 9, 208 pp, Quality PB, ISBN 1-893361-19-5 **$16.95**

What You Will See Inside a Mosque
by *Aisha Karen Khan;* full-color photographs by *Aaron Pepis*

A colorful, fun-to-read introduction that explains the ways and whys of Muslim faith and worship.

Through concise but enlightening description and full-page color photographs from North American mosques, this guide satisfies kids' curiosity about what goes on in mosques, broadens the awareness of other faiths, and provides Muslim children with a deeper understanding of the practices of their own religious tradition.
8½ x 10½, 32 pp, full-color illus., Hardcover, ISBN 1-893361-60-8 **$16.95**